GOD'S WORD
FOR A JR. HIGH WORLD

Prayer

Gospel Light

Darrell Pearson, Author
Kara Eckmann Powell, General Editor
Leader Article by Wayne Rice

1

Gospel Light is an evangelical Christian publisher dedicated to serving the local church. We believe God's vision for Gospel Light is to provide church leaders with biblical, user-friendly materials that will help them evangelize, disciple and minister to children, youth and families.

We hope this Gospel Light resource will help you discover biblical truth for your own life and help you minister to youth. God bless you in your work.

For a free catalog of resources from Gospel Light please contact your Christian supplier or contact us at 1-800-4-GOSPEL *or at* www.gospellight.com.

PUBLISHING STAFF
William T. Greig, Publisher
Dr. Elmer L. Towns, Senior Consulting Publisher
Dr. Gary S. Greig, Senior Consulting Editor
Jill Honodel, Managing Editor
Pam Weston, Editor
Patti PenningtonVirtue, Assistant Editor
Christi Goeser, Editorial Assistant
Kyle Duncan, Associate Publisher
Bayard Taylor, M.Div., Senior Editor, Theological and Biblical Issues
Kevin Parks, Cover Designer
Debi Thayer, Designer
Wayne Rice and Donna Fitzpatrick, Contributing Writers

ISBN 0-8307-2408-7
© 1999 by Gospel Light
All rights reserved.
Printed in U.S.A.

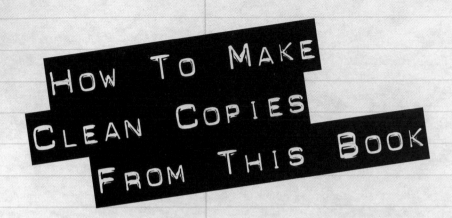

PRAISE FOR PULSE

"**There is a cry from this generation for Truth.**" Helen Musick, Youth Specialties National Resource Team member, national speaker and author

"**The Pulse curriculum is truly cross-cultural.**" Walt Mueller, President, Center for Parent/Youth Understanding and author of *Understanding Today's Youth Culture*

"**The creators and writers of this curriculum know and love young teens, and that's what sets [this] curriculum apart from the mediocre stuff!**" Mark Oestreicher, Vice President of Ministry Resources, Youth Specialties

"**Great biblical material, creative interaction and USER FRIENDLY! What more could you ask? I highly recommend it!**" Ken Davis, President, Dynamic Communications International

"**It's about time...curriculum took [junior highers] and...youth workers seriously.**" Rich Van Pelt, Strategic Relationships Director, Compassion International, author, speaker and veteran youth worker

"**A rich resource...that makes genuine connections with middle school students and the culture in which they must live.**" Mark W. Cannister, Ed.D., Chair, Department of Youth Ministries, Gordon College

"**A fresh tool...geared to make a lasting impact.**" Paul Fleischmann, Executive Director, National Network of Youth Ministries

"**This is the best I've seen yet.**" Wayne Rice, author and Junior High Ministry Director, Understanding Your Teenager seminars

"**A landmark resource for years to come.**" Chapman R. Clark, Ph.D., Associate Professor of Youth and Family Ministry, Fuller Theological Seminary

"**It fleshes out...two absolute essentials for great curriculum: biblical depth and active learning.**" Duffy Robbins, Associate Professor, Department of Youth Ministry, Eastern College

"**Pulse...will help God's Word to become real for your students.**" Larry Acosta, President, The Hispanic Ministry Center

"**Pulse will help leaders...bring excellence to every lesson while enjoying the benefit of a simplified preparation time.**" Lynn Ziegenfuss, Vice President of People Development, Youth for Christ/USA

"**Pulse CAPITALIZES both God and Truth.**" Monty L. Hipp, Youth Communicator, Creative Communications

"**The best junior high/middle school curriculum to come out in years.**" Jim Burns, Ph.D., President, National Institute of Youth Ministry

"**Wow! I'm impressed with the quality and message this curriculum brings to the millennials.**" Charles Kim, *JDM—Journey Devotional Magazine*, The Oriental Mission Church

Pulse Prayer

CONTENTS CONTENTS CONTENTS CONTENTS CONTENTS

The Ten Top Reasons... 8
Moving Through Pulse 10
It's Your Move   Me? Teach Junior Highers to Pray? By Wayne Rice 13
Contributors 14

Unit I: Big Truths About Prayer

Session One   Prayer Is a Direct Line to God 15
            Prayer is a two-way conversation with God.
            There's no call-waiting or being put on hold!

Session Two   Roadblocks Hinder Our Prayers 31
            In order to talk to God effectively, we have to overcome some
            tough roadblocks.

Session Three   God Has Given a Pattern for Prayer 43
            Praying is much more than just asking God for help

Unit II: Big Questions About Prayer

Session Four   What Can I Do When Prayer Gets Boring? 59
            Since prayer has many forms, we can talk to God in all sorts of different ways.

Session Five   Does God *Always* Answer Prayers? 73
            God answers every prayer in His own timing and in His own way.

Session Six   Why Do We Have to Keep On Praying? 83
            Persistence and practice are good things—especially when it comes to praying.

On the Move   How Do I Pray? 95

Dedication

To Hilary, named
for great mountain
climbers and great
happiness, Thanks
for showing me
That one can live
The abundant life—
even while in
middle school.

-Dad

....You've Made the Right Choice in Choosing Pulse for Your Junior Highers

The Top Ten Reasons...

9. Junior highers need and deserve youth workers who are expert trainers and teachers of biblical truth.

Every book is pulsating with youth leader tips and a full-length youth worker article designed to infuse YOU with more passion and skill for your ministry to junior highers.

10. Junior highers equate who God is with what church is like. To them a boring youth ministry means a boring God.

Fun and variety are the twin threads that weave their way through this curriculum's every page.

8. Junior highers need ongoing reminders of the big idea of each session.

Wouldn't it be great if you could give your students devotionals every week to reinforce the learning goals of the session? Get this: YOU CAN because THIS CURRICULUM DOES.

7. Some of our world's most effective evangelists are junior highers.

Every session, and we mean EVERY session, concludes with an evangelism option that ties "the big idea" of the session to the big need to share Christ with others.

6. Since no two junior highers (or their leaders) look, think or act alike, no two junior high ministries look, think or act alike.

Each step comes with three options that you can cut and paste to create a session that works best for YOUR students and YOUR personality.

5. Junior highers' growing minds are ready for more than just fun and games with a little Scripture thrown in.

Scripture is the very skeleton of each session, giving it its shape, its form and its very life.

4. Junior highers learn best when they can see, taste, feel and experience the session.

This curriculum involves students in every step through active learning and games to prove to students that following Christ is the greatest adventure ever.

3. Tragically, most junior highers are under challenged in their walks with Christ.

We've packed the final step of each session with three options that serve to move students a few steps forward in their walks with Christ.

2. Junior highers tend to understand the Bible in bits and pieces and miss the big picture of all that God has done for them.

This curriculum follows a strategic three-year plan that walks junior highers through the Bible, stopping at the most important points along the way.

1. Junior highers are moving through all sorts of changes—from getting a new body to getting a new locker.

We've designed a curriculum that revolves around one simple vision: Moving God's Word into a junior high world.

Moving Through Pulse

Since Pulse is vibrating with so many different learning activities, this guide will help you pick and choose the best possible options for *your* students.

THE SESSIONS

The six sessions are split into two stand-alone units, so you can choose to teach either three or six sessions at a time. Each session is geared to be 45 to 90 minutes long and is comprised of the following four steps.

IT'S YOUR MOVE

A training article for you, the youth worker, to show you *why* and *how* to see students' worlds changed by Christ to change the world.

STEP 1 — MOVING IN

This first step helps students focus in on the theme of the lesson in a fun and engaging way through three options:

 MOVE IT—An active learning experience that may or may not involve all of your students.

 CHAT ROOM—Provocative, clear and simple questions to get your students thinking and chatting.

 FUN AND GAMES—Zany, creative and competitive games that may or may not involve all of your students.

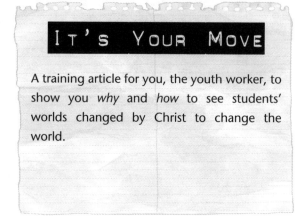

STEP 2 — MOVING UP

The second step enables students to look up to God by relating the very words of Scripture to the session topic through three options:

 MOVE IT—An active learning experience that may or may not involve all of your students.

 CHAT ROOM—Provocative, clear and simple questions to get your students chatting about the Scripture lesson.

 PULSE POINTS—A message outline with simple points and meaningful illustrations to give students some massive truths about Scripture with hardly any preparation on your part.

STEP 3
MOVING ON

STEP 4
MOVING OUT

This step asks students to look inward and discover how God's Word connects with their own worlds through three options:

CHAT ROOM—Provocative, clear and simple questions to get your students chatting.

REAL LIFE—A case study about someone (usually a junior higher) who needs your students' help figuring out what to do.

TOUGH QUESTIONS—Four to six mind-stretching questions that challenge students to a new level of depth and integration.

This final step leads students out into their world with specific challenges to apply at school, at home and with their friends through three options based on your students' growth potential:

LIGHT THE FIRE—For junior highers who may or may not be Christians and need easily accessible application ideas.

FIRED UP—For students who are definitely Christians and are ready for more intense application ideas.

SPREAD THE FIRE—A special evangelism application idea for students with a passion to see others come to know Christ.

OTHER IMPORTANT MOVING PARTS

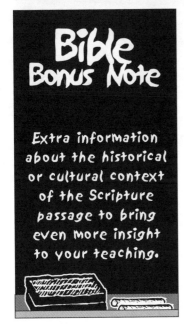

Bible Bonus Note

Extra information about the historical or cultural context of the Scripture passage to bring even more insight to your teaching.

Youth Leader Tip

Suggestions, options and/or other useful information to make your life easier or at least more interesting!

Devotions in Motion
WEEK FIVE: GRACE

Four devotionals for each session to keep the big idea moving through your junior highers' lives all week long.

ON THE MOVE—An appealing, easy-to-read handout you can give your junior highers to make sure they learn all the basics of Prayer.

Heads Up Tips:

Session 2 calls for the video *Putting Your Real Heart Forward* from Youth Specialties' Live the Life series. You can order the video directly from Youth Specialties at 1-800-776-8008.

Session 2, Step 4 calls for several Bibles to give away. It's a good idea to keep "give away" Bibles on hand for students who don't have one of their own or those who have just made the decision to dedicate their lives to Christ (maybe because of you!).Inexpensive Bibles can be purchased through the American Bible Society (http://www.americanbible.org).

Session 6 refers to the book *Practice the Presence of God* by Brother Lawrence (Washington, D.C.: ICS Publications, 1994).You can find this book at any Christian book store.

Prayer

Me? Teach Junior Highers to Pray?

Hey kids! Guess what our next study topic is going to be?

Demons and witchcraft?

No and no.

Famous love scenes from the Bible (giggle, giggle)?

Sorry.

How about rock music! Yeah, cool! Rock 'n' roll!

Wrong again, pop music lovers. Actually, our next topic will be...

PRAYER!

If what you hear next is moaning and whining about how boring and irrelevant both you and your topic are, don't despair. That means your junior high ministry is ready for a study on prayer. Obviously they have no idea what an exciting and powerful thing prayer really is—and you get to teach them all about it. Consider yourself lucky.

I know you don't feel very lucky. Prayer is, after all, a serious spiritual topic and junior highers are rarely serious or spiritual even on their best days. On top of that, prayer is something of a mystery—not easily explained to adults, let alone to young adolescents. True. But junior highers are nevertheless ready and anxious to learn about prayer. In fact, they are at the perfect age for learning how to pray.

Why? Three reasons:

1. Junior highers are in transition. Just as they are changing physically and intellectually from childhood to adulthood, so they are changing spiritually. They are acquiring a faith of their own that is more personal, more relationship-centered than ever before. For the first time, they are ready to experience God as a personal friend and confidant,

It's Your Move

someone they can talk with and listen to. Prayer is the language of this new relationship and junior highers are eager to learn it.

2. Junior highers love to be active participants in everything, and prayer is one way they can be involved in what God is doing. Prayer is not a passive religious exercise—something you say before a meal or after a sermon—but a dynamic means for invoking the power of God. Junior highers make very effective prayer warriors because they love putting their growing relationship with Christ into action.

3. Junior highers have a tremendous need for affirmation and respect. As they grow into adulthood, they crave people who will take time to listen to them and take their feelings and ideas seriously. Prayer, of course, is God's way of saying to a junior higher—as well as to you and me—"Come, let's sit down and talk. I have all the time in the world. I want to listen to you."

Prayer is the lifeblood of faith. Without it, faith inevitably dies. That's why your junior highers need to learn to pray. Don't worry if they don't understand everything about prayer. Who does? Just help them understand that God wants them to pray. Let them know that God wants to listen to them. He is interested in them and what they have to say.

The best way to teach this, of course, is to model it. If you listen to them, they just might come to believe that God will listen to them too.

Wayne Rice,
Director of Understanding Your Teenager
Author of *Junior High Ministry*

Wayne Rice is a founding member of Youth Specialties, author of Junior High Ministry and president of Understanding Your Teenager.

Contributors

Donna Fitzpatrick, author of the student article, "How Do I Pray?" lives in Northern California with her husband, Dan, and seven of her eight children. With the oldest in her third year of college and the youngest in her third year of age, life is never dull! Donna enjoys writing, public speaking and home schooling.

 Prayer

The Big Idea

Prayer is a two-way conversation with God. There's no call-waiting or being put on hold!

Session Aims

In this session you will guide students to:

- Know that God hears them when they pray;
- Discover their need to spend time communicating with God;
- Commit to carving a few minutes out of their schedules this week to communicate with God.

The Biggest Verse

"This poor man called, and the Lord heard him; he saved him out of all his troubles." Psalm 34:6

Other Important Verses

Psalms 34:1-8,15-18; 91:4; 119:105; Isaiah 60:1-5

CALL BOX

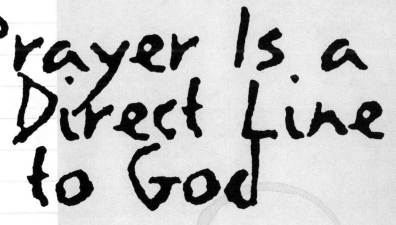

Prayer Is a Direct Line to God

This step introduces the idea that prayer is communication with God.

Option 1  Move It

Video Option

You'll need A video camera and a TV.

Ahead of time, have a team of several students and one adult volunteer prepare a video, asking questions about prayer of various people during the week before the meeting. Instruct the team to ask simple questions such as: *What do you think prayer is? When do you pray? When was the last time you prayed? Should you close your eyes every time you pray?*

Open the meeting by showing the video, then ask: **How would you define prayer?** Explain: **Prayer can be defined in three words: communication with God. By the time we finish this session, you'll know the definition of prayer for sure.**

Impromptu Interview Option

You'll need A portable tape recorder (or several, if you can get them), several notepads and pens or pencils.

Greet students and explain that today each of them will become newspaper and TV reporters. Divide students into teams of two or three and distribute the tape recorder(s), notepads and pens or pencils. Instruct students to approach several people outside the classroom, asking simple questions during their interviews, such as: *What do you think prayer is? When do you pray? When was the last time you prayed? Should you close your eyes every time you pray?*

After 5 to 10 minutes of information gathering, have students return to report to the group what they discovered. See if they can make any general conclusions about people's thoughts on prayer by discussing the following:

Were people comfortable talking about prayer?
How do people generally define prayer?
How often do they pray?

Ask: **How would you define prayer?** Explain: **Prayer can be defined in three words: communication with God. By the time we finish this session, you'll know the definition of prayer for sure.**

Option 2 — Chat Room

You'll need Zippo!

Greet students warmly, then ask the following questions:

Has anyone here ever met or seen someone famous? Tell us about it.

Do you know this person well from this encounter? Probably not!

Who do you know really well? Tell us about that person.

How did you get to know that person so well?

Explain: **Today we're going to talk about a thing called prayer, the way to get to know someone really famous—God. What do you think prayer is?** Follow up by explaining: **Prayer can be defined in three words: communication with God.**

Explain that you're going to read several statements and that students should raise their thumbs and point them up if they agree, point them down if they disagree and point them sideways if they're not sure.

Talking to God is easy.

Prayer is comfortable for me.

Prayer should be hard to do since God is so awesome.

I've heard God talk to me.

I know God talks to other people.

I've heard my goldfish talk to me.

Prayer is mainly done in church.

Prayer happens mainly when people are scared or desperate.

Prayer happens most often right before math tests at my school.

Prayer happens most often when math test results come out as report cards.

Explain: **Today we're going to start a new series on prayer, and it will definitely change what you think about prayer.**

Option 3 — Fun and Games

You'll need A silly prize (for example, a trophy from a thrift store) and a watch with a seconds indicator.

Introduce this session by explaining that you're going to start with a competition to see who is the best and most creative talker in the group. Show students the incredible prize (or maybe you should keep the incredible prize a secret so you'll get volunteers!), then ask for two volunteers at a time to compete against each other. Each person comes to the front and is given a topic to discuss. They each have 30 seconds to talk about what they know. Explain that even if they don't know much about the topic, the key is to keep talking for the entire 30 seconds! After several contestants have talked, pick the top two for the championship.

Round One
Contestant 1: **Explain the toughest things about being a junior higher.**
Contestant 2: **Tell us the biggest problems with teachers today.**

Round Two
Contestant 3: **Describe the history of bowling in America.**
Contestant 4: **Explain step-by-step how cars are made.**

Round Three
Contestant 5: **Tell us what visitors should expect to find when visiting China.**
Contestant 6: **Explain why dogs like to ride with their heads sticking out the car windows.**

Now choose the two best contestants to go against each other in the final round.

Championship Round Four
Contestant 1: **Tell us everything you know about prayer.**
Contestant 2: **Describe the different methods people use to talk to God.**

Have students vote for the champion talker. Give the champ the incredible prize, then explain: **The key definition for prayer can be summarized in three words: communication with God. For the next few minutes you are going to learn even more about what prayer and talking to God are all about.**

STEP **2** MOVING UP

This step helps motivate students to pray by helping them realize that God hears them.

Option 1 **Move It**

You'll need Several Bibles, a watch with a seconds indicator, several copies of "Lack of Listening" (p. 24) copied on one color of paper, several copies of "Lots of Listening" (p. 25) copied on a *different color* of paper .

Ahead of time, cut the two sets of copies into separate cards.

Distribute the cards to students, making sure that there is an even number of each color distributed. Ask students not to show anyone what their cards say. If anyone asks why they're different colors, reply with something vague, such as, "You'll see." Instruct students to find someone who has a different color card from theirs and pair up. Once students have paired up, give them 20 seconds to do whatever their card tells them to. After 20 seconds, ask students to switch cards with someone else who has their same color, then find a new partner who has the opposite color card. Allow 20 seconds again for the students to do whatever the cards tell them to do. Repeat one or two more times, then ask students to return to their seats.

Debrief the experience by asking students to share what happened to them. Ask: **Did anyone figure out the difference between the two colors of cards?** Since junior highers often feel like they're not being listened to, ask: **How does it feel not to be listened to?** You may want to share a story from your own life, especially while you were in junior high, when you felt that someone was not listening to you and how frustrating that was.

Explain: **There is only one Person you know who will listen to you all the time, and this whole series is about having a conversation with that Person.** Ask volunteers to read Psalm 34:1-8.

Continue: **Verses 1 to 3 represent the commitment of the writer** (possibly David) **to continually praise God.**

More than that, in verse 3, the author encourages other people to join with him in celebrating God.

The reason for the praise is explained in verses 4 to 8. Read these verses aloud again, asking students to listen to all the words that the writer uses to describe God. Ask: **What phrases stand out in these verses?** Make sure to draw attention to verse 6, "This poor man called, and the LORD heard him; he saved him out of all his troubles." Continue: **In this verse, as in many of the psalms, "poor" doesn't mean not having money; it means someone knowing that what you have won't really save you— only God will.**

Now read Psalm 34:15-18, asking students to listen for the connection between these verses and the idea of being "poor" in verse 6. Allow them to comment, then explain: **God hears anyone who prays to Him, but these verses teach us that He is especially close to those who are right, or righteous, before Him, and those who know they need Him.** This would be a good time to explain what it means to be "righteous" before Him, meaning having asked Jesus to forgive our sin and take over our lives.

Combine w/ next pag

Option 2 **Chat Room**

You'll need Several Bibles, copies of "Give a Grade" (p. 26) and pens or pencils.

Explain: **As junior highers, you're used to being graded at school but you hardly ever get to give out any grades yourselves. We're going to change all that today.** Distribute copies of "Give a Grade" and pens or pencils to students and allow three minutes to give a listening grade to the people mentioned on the report card. They get to grade both on how available the people are and how well they listen when the students actually talk to them. After three minutes, ask:

Who got the highest grade for availability?

How about for listening well?

Who got the lowest grade for availability?

What about the lowest grade for listening well?

How do you feel when you're not listened to?

Explain: **Today we're going to learn about someone who would get an A+ both in being available *and* in being a good listener. That person is God Himself. But first we need to listen carefully to some words about Him.**

18

Read Psalm 34:1-8 and 15-18. Ask: **What does "radiant" mean? Why are some people "radiant"?** Because they have the kind of joy that comes from God and changes how they feel about life, the kind of joy also mentioned in Isaiah 60:1-5.

Does verse 6 mean that God just cares about people who don't have much money? No, God cares about people who are "poor" in their attitude toward Him, meaning they know how much they need Him, and that whatever they themselves have or can do won't save them.

Why would the writer, who is possibly David, say "taste and see that the Lord is good"? We can't actually taste God, can we? No, it's a metaphor to describe what it means to really get to know and experience God.

If a test said, "True or false: God has favorites," what would you answer? Tough question, especially when you read Psalm 34:15-18. God does love everyone, but He does seem to be especially close to those who are righteous and "crushed in spirit?"

What does it mean to be righteous and crushed in spirit? Being righteous means you are in right standing with God, which can happen only if you've asked His Son Jesus to come into your life and forgive your sin. Being crushed in spirit is like being "poor," meaning that you know how much you need God, and that you can't do much without Him.

Option 3  Pulse Points

You'll need Several Bibles, a table, a watch with a seconds indicator and three *each* of different kinds of candy bars.

Ahead of time, unwrap all the candy bars so you can lay them out on the table without any wrappers. Choose one kind of the candy and soak all three bars of that brand in some water and salt so that the salt saturates them, but doesn't disintegrate them.

To introduce this message, ask for three volunteers who would like to play "Name That Candy!" Have the three volunteers leave the room with another adult leader. Lay out the unwrapped candy on a table as you explain to the remaining students that the candy at the end of the table has been soaked in salt water.

One at a time, call the volunteers into the room and explain that you're going to time them to see how quickly they can Name That Candy! The contestant should proceed down the table, taking a bite of each candy, then giving its name. They can't say the name of the candy without first taking a bite, even if they think they know what it is. What you and the audience know is that when the contestants get to the end of the table, they'll be in for quite a surprise!

After all three volunteers have had their turn, have them sit down and explain: **Sometimes things that we think are going to taste bad are actually good and sometimes things that are supposed to taste good are actually bad. Today we're going to look at something, or rather Someone, who tastes good all the time. We never have to wonder if He's going to be good or not.**

Read Psalm 34:4-8;15-18 aloud and continue: **The writer knew God so well it was like he had tasted Him, and he wants us to taste and see God's goodness also. We can learn two things about the God who is good to us all the time from this passage.**

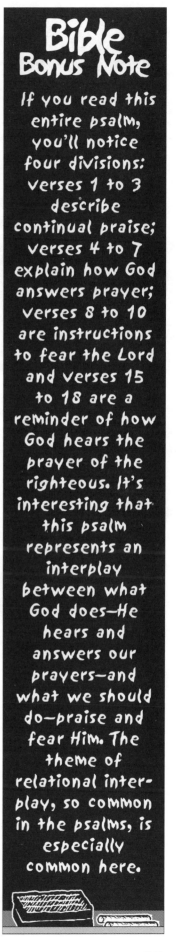

Bible Bonus Note

If you read this entire psalm, you'll notice four divisions: verses 1 to 3 describe continual praise; verses 4 to 7 explain how God answers prayer; verses 8 to 10 are instructions to fear the Lord and verses 15 to 18 are a reminder of how God hears the prayer of the righteous. It's interesting that this psalm represents an interplay between what God does—He hears and answers our prayers—and what we should do—praise and fear Him. The theme of relational interplay, so common in the psalms, is especially common here.

1. In His goodness, God hears our prayers.

Read Psalm 34:6 again. Explain: **God is big enough to hear all of us when we pray, even if we all pray at once.** Ask for two student volunteers who would like the chance to get some candy (no, not the salt-covered candy this time!). Once they come to the front of the room, ask everyone else to find a partner and begin talking to that partner about anything that they have done in the last two days. The two volunteers will be listening closely to see how many conversations they can actually hear and understand. After 30 seconds, ask the two volunteers to share the conversations that they heard. Odds are that they'll never be able to hear and understand all the conversations, but give a candy bar to the student who understood the most.

Explain: **God isn't like that. We can all talk to Him at once and He'll hear and understand us. As junior highers, you might be used to feeling like your parents, your brothers and sisters, your teachers, and sometimes even the adults at church don't listen to you. God** *always* **listens.**

2. God is good to those who know they need Him.

Read Psalm 34:15 and 18 again. Explain: **Although God hears everyone all the time, He seems especially attentive to people who know they need Him. Being "right-eous" means being "right" before God, which can only happen by asking His Son, Jesus Christ, to forgive our sin and bring us back into right relationship with Him. Being "crushed in spirit" means knowing that our own abilities and possessions leave us broken, and that only God can meet our needs.**

Illustration to further drive home the point: Give yet another candy bar as a loan to a student and explain that you're going to try asking her for it two different times. The first time you should act pretty tough, and explain that you don't really need the candy bar because you have your own food pretty well figured out on your own, but if she feels like it, she can give it to you. The second time you should act really needy, explaining that you have no way on your own to get a candy bar, and that without the candy bar, you'll really be in trouble. Ask her and the rest of the group what type of person would they be willing to give the candy bar to: the first tough person or the second needy person. Explain that the same is true with God. Our sense of neediness brings us even closer to Him.

Continue: **Recently a story was circulated that provides a penetrating picture of God's care for those who are helpless or needy.**

After a forest fire in Yellowstone National Park, forest rangers began their trek up a mountain to assess the inferno's damage. One ranger found a bird literally petrified in ashes, perched statuesquely on the ground at the base of a tree. Somewhat sickened by the eerie sight, he knocked over the bird with a stick. When he struck it, three tiny chicks scurried from under their dead mother's wings.

The loving mother, keenly aware of impending disaster, had carried her offspring to the base of the tree and had gathered them under her wings, instinctively knowing that the toxic smoke would rise. She could have flown to safety but had refused to abandon her babies. When the blaze had arrived and the heat had scorched her small body, the mother had remained steadfast. Because she had been willing to die, those under the cover of her wings would live.

"He will cover you with his feathers, and under his wings you will find refuge" (Psalm 91:4). Explain: **He hides us in the shadow of His wings. Have you ever watched a bird protect its young this way? God wraps Himself around us to protect us from harm and from people who might hurt us.**

STEP 3 MOVING ON

This step helps students feel their need to spend time communicating with God through prayer.

Option 1 Chat Room

You'll need Several Bibles, copies of "What's in a Friend?" (p. 27) and pens or pencils.

Give each student a copy of "What's in a Friend?" and a pen or pencil. Ask them to take three minutes and write a description of their best friend. When they're done, have several students read their descriptions to the group, then instruct everyone to turn their papers over and take another three minutes to write a description of God. When done, ask everyone to share a statement or two with the whole group. Ask:

What is God like?

What is He like to you?

Was it harder to write about God than about your friend? Why or why not?

Why do you know your friend so well?

Explain: **You probably know your friend well because you spend a lot of time together. That's how we get to know God as well—we spend time with Him. No doubt the writer of Psalm 34 had spent a lot of time with God, allowing him to experience His goodness. Who can tell us about a time when you felt like you really spent a great time with God? How did that happen? What happened during this special time with God?**

Continue: **Since God thinks so much of us, it's a natural response to want to spend time with Him in prayer. Prayer is nothing more than spending time with God, both talking *and* listening. Of course, in** addition to prayer, we already have something that helps us listen to God: the Bible. The Bible contains God's Word to us over several thousands of years, and yet it still speaks to us today. We learn in Psalm 119:105 that His Word is like a lamp to our feet and a light for our path. Reading it allows us to hear from God any time we want. We don't have to wait for a huge booming voice from heaven; we can hear from Him by opening the Book He has given to us.**

Option 2 Real Life

You'll need A volunteer mom or dad and their baby or toddler.

Ahead of time, arrange for the parent and the baby to be available for a live interview on the topic of what it's like to be a parent.

Introduce the parent and the baby to the students, then begin the interview by asking specifics about the baby's personality, behavior and characteristics. Why do they know so much about their baby? Then ask them about their relationship with God: What level of intimacy do they have with God? When do they spend time with Him? What do they do during this time? Have they ever felt like God was talking to them?

Wrap up the interview by explaining to the students: **Just like this baby and parent, we get to know our heavenly Father better as we spend time talking with Him and listening to Him through prayer. That's undoubtedly what the writer of Psalm 34 must have done in order to "taste and see" that God was good. Of course, in addition to prayer, we have something else that helps us listen to God: the Bible. The Bible contains our heavenly Father's word to us over several thousands of years, and yet it still speaks to us today. We learn in Psalm 119:105 that His Word is like a lamp to our feet and a light for our path. Reading God's Word allows us to hear from God any time we want. We don't have to wait for a huge booming voice from heaven; we can hear from our Father by opening the Book He has given to us.**

Option 3 — Tough Questions

You'll need Nothing, except the following questions!

Option: Print out the questions on a white board, chalkboard, an overhead transparency or a make a handout of the questions for small group discussions.

1. **Is it dangerous to be too friendly with God by being too buddy-buddy with Him instead of respecting His awesomeness?** No, God is big enough to be both our awesome Creator as well as our best personal Friend.

2. **Do you ever feel as if God really doesn't care about who you are? Why?** Lots of people feel this way sometimes, but the truth is that He always cares.

3. **Do you think people in the Bible had a closer relationship with God than we can have today? Why?** One of the reasons there are stories in the Bible of people talking with God is precisely because they were unique. In Moses' day, most people didn't talk to God like Moses did. Most people in history talked to God just like we do today—in prayer.

4. **Does God ever talk in an audible voice to people? Have you ever known anyone who experienced this? If not in an audible voice, how does He speak?** Yes, He still speaks every once in a while through a voice you can actually hear. He also speaks through a ton of other ways, like through Scripture passages, other people, our feelings or our circumstances.

NOTES

STEP

MOVING OUT

This step challenges students to commit to carving out a few minutes in their schedules this week to communicate with God.

Option: Purchase a bag of feathers at a craft store (or take apart an old feather pillow!) and hand feathers to students as they leave to remind them of Psalm 91:4: "He will cover you with his feathers, and under his wings you will find refuge."

Option 1  Light the Fire

You'll need Key chains or rings with one blank or old key on each to remind students to think about God and talk to Him.

Tell the students you're going to give them a little gift (and they say you never do anything for them!). After you pass out the key chains tell them to put theirs in a place where they'll discover it periodically during the week, such as their backpack, lunch box or pocket. Explain that every time they come across the key chain, you want them to stop for a brief moment, think about God and tell Him something about their day—just like they would to a friend. Bits of time with a friend—it's the key to knowing God!

Option 2  Fired Up

You'll need Friendship bracelets or W. W. J. D. (What Would Jesus Do) bracelets (which can be purchased at a local Christian bookstore or made with simple leather strips or yarn and beads).

Hand out the bracelets and have students put them on. Explain that these are a reminder to call a friend and remind her to pray. Have each of them choose a prayer buddy and challenge them to call their prayer buddies after school every day for the next week to remind them

to spend a moment praying to God. They can even choose to pray together over the phone.

Option 3  Spread the Fire

You'll need Card stock cut up to the size of business cards. You will need five cards for each student.

Hand out five small cards to each student. Instruct them to write the names of five people who they would like to see come to know God more intimately—a different name on each card. Challenge them to put the cards in a place where they'll find them frequently (such as a wallet or backpack) and to talk to God about these friends every time they come across the cards. Tell them to flip through each card and pray individually for each person. Let them know that during the week you're going to call them and see how they're doing. Then do it!

NOTES

Lack of Listening

Note to leader: Photocopy this page on one color of paper. Then cut cards apart.

You see something in the room that you find fascinating and you can't stop talking about it.

You walk off and leave while your partner is talking to you.

You constantly interrupt as your partner is trying to talk to you.

You close your eyes, cross your arms and act bored.

You sing as your partner is talking to you.

No matter what your partner talks to you about, you talk about something totally different that has absolutely no connection with what he or she is saying.

Lots of Listening

Note to leader: Photocopy this page on a different color of paper. Then cut cards apart.

Share a story about something that scared you.

Tell your partner about the best thing that happened to you this week.

Tell your partner what you would buy if you were given a million dollars.

Tell your partner about your favorite things to do after school.

Share about your favorite foods with your partner.

Tell your partner about your school, your teachers and your classes.

Give a Grade

Here's your big chance to give a grade to some people you know. Think about how available the following people are to listen to you, then give them a grade based on how well they listen once you actually talk with them. You can give them an A, B, C, D or F.

For instance, your dad might be really busy and hardly ever available to talk to, in which case you might give him a C for availability; but when you do get the chance to talk to him, he listens really well, in which case he'd get an A for listening well.

Your name_____ DaTe _____

NAME	How available are They?					How well do They listen?				
	A	B	C	D	F	A	B	C	D	F
Mom										
STepmom										
Dad										
STepdad										
BroTher										
SisTer										
FavoriTe Teacher										
LeasT favoriTe Teacher										
ClosesT friend										
AdulTs aT church										

What's in a Friend?

Write a description of your closest friend.

nice, kind, sometimes mean, sometimes nice, owns a

pet pig, tall, short, loves God, likes to play Parcheesi, a good li

stener, my same age, friendly, owns cool computer, games, encourages me, helps me with problems, tells great jokes

Devotions in Motion

DAY 1

FAST FACTS

Dive into Jeremiah 29:11-13 to learn more about what it means to have a two-way conversation with God through prayer.

God Says

You're trying to explain your great plan for Friday night to your friend Jung, and you're starting to get a little frustrated. You're telling him about the cool overnighter you've got planned, complete with ice cream sundaes and the new computer game you just got from your parents, and all Jung is doing is listening to music and ignoring you. Well, lots of times when God is trying to tell us this great plans, we follow Jung's example and ignore Him.

I Do

There is no better plan for you than God's plan. Take five minutes to seek God with your whole heart, asking Him to show you this plan.

FOLD HERE

DAY 4

QUICK QUESTIONS

Turn toward the end of your Bible to see what James 2:23 has to say to you today.

God Says

Who is your closest friend in the world?

How have you gotten to know this friend better this last month? Try to think of at least four things you've learned about your friend.

Abraham is called a friend of God. How do you think Abraham's friendship with God is similar to your friendship with your closest friend?

☐ Abraham and God play basketball together although God always seems to win.

☐ Abraham and God spend time talking.

☐ Abraham and God watch TV together.

☐ Abraham and God skateboard to school together.

I Do

What is one way you can develop your friendship with God today?

© 1999 by Gospel Light. Permission to photocopy granted. *Prayer*

QUICK QUESTIONS

To find out more about how prayer builds your friendship with God, check out Jeremiah 33:2,3.

God Says

What does God promise He'll do for us if we call to Him?

What are some of the great and mighty things God will tell us as we pray?

☐ The number of skateboards that would need to be stacked on top of one another to reach the moon?

☐ The cure for bad-hair days?

☐ The recipe for M&Ms?

☐ All of the above?

☐ None of the above?

I Do

God could tell us anything, but usually He tells us exciting things about Himself. What do you think God is telling you about Himself today?

FOLD HERE -

FAST FACTS

Don't wait another second before you turn to Psalm 27:10.

God Says

Alone. That's the only word to describe how you feel. Your dad divorced your mom two years ago and now he lives clear across the country. Your mom is out on a date with her new boyfriend. Your older sister is in her bedroom but cares more about talking on the phone to her friends than about talking to you. Sitting on your bed in your room you feel like you have no one to talk to. No one to talk to except God that is. God is always ready to welcome you.

I Do

It's typical for teenagers to feel alone. But the good news is that you're really not alone. God is always waiting to have a conversation with you, even when no one else is. You can talk to Him at any time and in any place. You can talk to Him out loud, in a whisper or in your thoughts. You can tell Him exactly how you feel

Pulse Prayer

The Big Idea

In order to talk to God effectively, we have to overcome some tough roadblocks.

Session Aims

In this session you will guide students to:

- Identify the tough roadblocks to prayer, including those that are the most difficult for them personally;
- Understand Christ's love and acceptance for them even though they're not perfect;
- Commit to breaking down roadblocks in their own prayer lives.

The Biggest Verse

"Watch and pray so that you will not fall into temptation. The spirit is willing, but the body is weak." Matthew 26:41

Other Important Verses

Psalm 51:16,17; Matthew 26:17-75; John 21:15-17

Roadblocks Hinder Our Prayers

STEP

MOVING IN

This step introduces the idea that prayer is difficult for students because roadblocks get in the way.

Option 1  Move It

You'll need A VCR, a TV and the video *Putting Your Real Heart Forward* from the Live the Life series with Youth Specialties (1-800-776-8008). The video segment is called "So You Want to Be a Christian" and is a take-off on *Leave It to Beaver*, poking fun at the myth of the perfect Christian. **Note:** You may want to use the second video segment when you get to step 3, option 2.

Introduce the video by explaining (tongue-in-cheek) that you've finally discovered a great model for becoming a true Christian. Tell the group that the video shows not only how to live the Christian life, but how to integrate prayer into everyday life.

After the video, discuss the following:

What do you think about Brad's life?

Could you pray in the lunchroom like he did?

Does prayer come easily to you like it does to Brad?

Discuss the reality of prayer versus the fake scene, explaining: **Unlike Brad, most of us struggle with prayer because there are a lot of roadblocks to being a person of prayer.**

Option 2  Chat Room

You'll need Copies of "It's Tough to Pray" (p. 38) and pens or pencils.

Explain that as you read statements describing different activities, students are to choose which of the two activities is tougher to do. If they think the first thing you read is tougher, they should move to the left side of the room. If they think the second thing you read is tougher, they should move to the right side of the room. Ask:

Which is tougher to do...

Eat a shoelace or tie your friend's shoes with your teeth?

Write a history essay or do a science fair project?

Mow the lawn or vacuum the carpet?

Find a good snack in the refrigerator or find a good show on television?

Get your teeth cleaned or clean your room?

Have to go to the bathroom for over two hours on a long car trip or be jam-packed in a minivan for a two-week family vacation?

Pray or empty the dishwasher?

Transition by sharing how tough prayer can be sometimes and how it is easy to feel guilty about not praying enough. Then distribute the "It's Tough to Pray" handouts and pens or pencils. Give students a few minutes to complete them.

When students are done, divide them into groups of four or five and have them share their answers. Then bring the whole group back together and have students make conclusions about which roadblocks are the most common in the group.

Option 3  Fun and Games

You'll need A six-foot wall or other obstacle to climb over.

Ahead of time, using stacks of chairs, mattresses or tables (or a combination of them all), construct the roadblock.

Option: Call a local school and borrow a couple of large "crash pads," the kind that high-jumpers or gymnasts use, or do the activity outside using a block wall or a cargo net strung between two poles, or playground equipment.

Caution: Make sure the roadblock you build is structurally safe. Be inventive, but don't take unnecessary risks!

Divide students into groups of 10. Explain that the goal of the game is for each group to get as many people as they can to the other side, but there is a major roadblock in the way. Give each team two minutes to see how many people they can get over the roadblock. If they all get over, they can keep sending more over the wall for extra points. Rotate teams until each team has had a chance. If you have time, give each team a second chance to see if their score improves. When they've finished, discuss: **Who had the best method for getting people over? What was the toughest thing about the roadblock?** Transition to the next step by sharing: **Today's focus is on the tough roadblocks that prevent us from talking to God.**

STEP 2 MOVING UP

This step helps students understand that even Jesus' disciples had roadblocks to praying.

Option 1 Move It

You'll need Your Bible, carpet on the floor, soft music in the background, a Bible, several candles and something to read that will be pretty boring such as an article about the stock market or the government in Sri Lanka.

Settle the group down and have students find a place on the floor by themselves (at least two feet away from any other student). Ask them to lie down on their backs and get comfortable because you are going to read a story. Light the candles, start the music and turn the lights off. Read the article using a soothing and relaxed voice. When you're done, turn the lights on and have everyone sit up. Ask them: **Who found it hard to listen? Did anyone's mind start to wander? What made it so easy to drift away?** Now have everyone lie down again and repeat the process, but this time read Matthew 26:17-56. When you finish reading, have everybody sit up again and ask them if they were able to visualize the garden scene. Discuss:

What happened? Why?

Does it seem strange that the disciples couldn't keep awake to pray at such a crucial time? Why?

What were the main roadblocks to their prayers?

Conclude by explaining: **The disciples were real people like us. They had a hard time focusing on prayer because they had roadblocks as well. In addition to sleep, what are some other roadblocks to prayer?**

Note: If you're not going to use Option 1, in the Moving On Step 3, (pp. 35-36) make sure that you discuss the obstacles it addresses.

NOTES

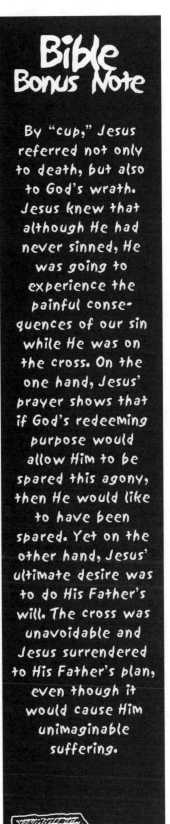

Bible Bonus Note

By "cup," Jesus referred not only to death, but also to God's wrath. Jesus knew that although He had never sinned, He was going to experience the painful consequences of our sin while He was on the cross. On the one hand, Jesus' prayer shows that if God's redeeming purpose would allow Him to be spared this agony, then He would like to have been spared. Yet on the other hand, Jesus' ultimate desire was to do His Father's will. The cross was unavoidable and Jesus surrendered to His Father's plan, even though it would cause Him unimaginable suffering.

Option 2 — Chat Room

You'll need Several Bibles, copies of "The Match Game" (p. 39) and pens or pencils.

Distribute "The Match Game" and pens or pencils to students. Instruct them to find other students who match them in the categories on the handout. Allow three or four minutes to make as many matches as they can, then have students sit down.

Explain: **Just as we have a lot more in common with each other than we might think, today's story is about people who have a lot in common with us. They are not other-worldly, super-spiritual people, but flesh and blood like us.** Distribute Bibles and ask a volunteer to read Matthew 26:30-46. Discuss the following:

Someone describe what happened on this night. What's the setting?

Was Jesus frustrated with his friends? Why?

Why couldn't the disciples stay awake?

How do you think Peter felt after what he declared in verse 35?

Have you ever found it hard to stay awake when you were supposed to be praying? Why?

Do you think you would have been like the disciples?

Even Jesus struggled in His prayer. What did He struggle with in His prayer? How did He resolve this struggle? What does this say to us today?

Ask: **In addition to sleep, what are some other roadblocks to prayer?** Being too busy or lazy, forgetting, thinking that it's not important or God already knows what we want, etc.

Option 3 — Pulse Points

You'll need Several Bibles and a bag of Oreo cookies.

>
> **Caution:** To avoid any potential embarrassment, it would be best if this student was of average weight.

Ask for a student volunteer who likes to eat Oreo cookies. Make up a name for this student, such as Mortimer, and explain: **Mortimer had a new goal: He wanted to eat more healthily. But Mortimer's one big obstacle to his goal was that he loved Oreo cookies. He loved them *so* much that any time he even heard one mentioned, he just had to eat one.**

Like Mortimer, often we start out with goals and we really mean to keep them, but then something gets in our way of meeting them. Read Matthew 26:31-35 and continue: **Peter's big goal was to follow Christ, but we'll see that there were a few roadblocks that got in Peter's way.** Read Matthew 26:36-46 and explain that we learn two truths about the roadblocks that stood in Peter's way.

1. Lots of things.

Explain: **Something as simple as sleep kept Peter from following Christ and doing what Christ wanted him to do, in this case pray. Here Peter makes a big declaration**

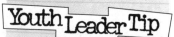

Often times in junior high ministry, laughing equals learning. Because of junior highers' concrete thinking skills, they'll most likely remember anything they see, especially if it provokes a memorable emotional response. Two weeks from now, the only thing they may remember from your talk will be Mortimer eating Oreo cookies. That's OK. That will trigger in them the story of Peter and their own similarities as people who often let roadblocks get in the way of their times of prayer.

about wanting to follow Christ and later that night, Peter blows it. It's probably pretty obvious that Jesus is going through a tough prayer time and yet Peter keeps falling asleep.

Call attention back to Mortimer. Explain that Mortimer had the goal of eating more healthy food, but every time he heard the word "Oreo," he couldn't help but eat an Oreo cookie. Starting now, instruct Mortimer to eat an Oreo cookie each time he hears the word "Oreo." At this point, make up a few sentences, such as: *An Oreo was Mortimer's biggest obstacle. Sure, there were others, but the Oreo cookie was the real enemy. It wasn't Mortimer's fault; it was the Oreo's!*

Continue: **In our lives, there's more than just an Oreo cookie that keeps us from praying** (yes, Mortimer should have eaten another cookie at this point).

> **Note:** If you're not going to use Option 1 in the Moving On Step 3 (pp. 35-36), you should address the roadblocks it contains here.

2. Lots of times.

Explain: **Peter allowed his prayer roadblock—sleep—to get in his way not just once or twice, but three times. Here Jesus Himself asks Peter to stay awake and pray and he can't do it. He fails repeatedly. The same is true in our lives. We allow these roadblocks to get in our way day after day after day.**

To illustrate, make up a story such as: **On Monday, Mortimer was going to eat a bucket of carrots, but then he saw those Oreos, and** *had* **to have one. Actually, he had two. (Is Mortimer keeping up?) On Tuesday, he was going to have a fruit smoothie, but he saw his little brother eating an Oreo and just** *had* **to have one himself.** The point is to get students laughing at Mortimer trying to eat cookies so quickly and make a visual point of how we are like Mortimer, who is like Peter, and we keep allowing other things to get in the way of a commitment to prayer.

This step enables students to identify specific roadblocks that they personally need to overcome.

You'll need Seven 2x2-foot poster boards.

Ahead of time, cut each poster board into the shape of a stop sign and write each of the following letters and words on a separate sign, placing the word underneath the letter: *A*—Anger, *B*—Busyness, *C*—Concentration, *D*—Doubt, *E*—Excuses, *F*—Forgetfulness, *G*—Good Times.

> **Note:** The seven signs can be used again in Option 1, Step 4.

Explain: **There are** *seven* **key roadblocks to prayer that affect us all at one time or another, keeping us from praying to God effectively.** Hold up the first sign: "*A*—Anger." **Sometimes we are angry at God and it keeps us from talking to Him, just like our anger sometimes keeps us from talking with a friend.** Continue with each letter, describing the roadblock and getting responses and illustrations from the students.

B—**Busyness:** We're often too busy for God.

C—**Concentration:** We try to pray, but our thoughts wander.

D—**Doubt:** We have times when we wonder if God is really out there listening.

E—**Excuses:** What are some great excuses we use to not pray?

F—**Forgetfulness:** I meant to pray, but…

G—**Good Times:** When things are going well, too often we don't pay any attention to God. When the bad times come, we're super pray-ers again.

Conclude by asking students to identify which of the seven roadblocks is their main obstacle to praying. Explain: **Many of these obstacles, if not all of them, are related to the way we miss the mark of what God wants. That's called sin and it gets in the way of having a relationship with God in general and in our prayer times specifically.**

Note: Only use this option if you used Option 1 in Step 1.

Option 2 — Real Life

You'll need A TV, a VCR and the video *Putting Your Real Heart Forward* from the Live the Life series with Youth Specialties.

Ahead of time, cue the video to the segment just after the "So You Want to Be a Christian" segment previously used in step 1.

Introduce the video by explaining: **Earlier we looked at the perfect Christian, our friend Brad. Let's take another look as he gets past his main roadblock—not being honest about who he really is.**

When the video clip is finished, ask:

Is Brad's relationship with God perfect?

What's the truth about Brad?

Do you think God would rather talk with Brad when he's being real or when he's acting perfect? Why?

Explain: **Brad seems afraid of letting others know about his problems. What Brad doesn't realize is that we all have a major problem and that problem is called sin. In the Bible, sin means missing the mark of what God wants us to do. Sin gets in the way of having a relationship with Him and spending time with Him in prayer. What God wants instead is the attitude in Psalm 51:16,17 of being brokenhearted about our sin and knowing our need for God's mercy. In fact, almost every obstacle that we've talked about so far is ultimately some sort of sin because it shows that we're not doing what God would want us to be doing.**

Option 3 — Tough Questions

You'll need Several Bibles and these questions!

Option: Use the questions in small group discussions by writing questions on the board, an overhead transparency or prepare a handout.

1. **Why is it hard to talk to God after we've sinned?** Because we are ashamed of our sins in comparison to God's perfection. But that's why Jesus came—to give us a path to God, even though we're imperfect.

2. **Why would Jesus pray to God that He wouldn't have to go through the crucifixion? Does that make Jesus seem less than God?** No, but it emphasizes His humanity. He struggled just like we do. That's why He can understand us so well.

3. **Read Matthew 26:47-75. How do you suppose Peter felt about letting Jesus down? Was it hopeless for Peter?** Read John 21:15-17. **Did his failure keep him permanently from Jesus?** No, even though he let Jesus down, Peter went on to become a main leader in the Early Church.

4. **Why do different people experience different obstacles?** God has made us all different. Some people have a hard time focusing because they're used to being busy, while others have a hard time setting aside the time to pray because they're pretty lazy and would rather watch TV or play on their computers. Lots of times it's our personalities and the kinds of lives that we live that cause different obstacles at different times.

5. **What's the biggest obstacle of all?** Our sin is the biggest obstacle of all. By sin, the Bible means missing the mark of what God wants us to do. Almost every obstacle we've talked about so far can ultimately be described as sin because they are not the things that God wants us to be doing.

6. **What's the difference between sin and sins?** Well, it's more than just one little *s* at the end of the word. Sin is our condition of being spiritually dead. This causes us to commit lots of *sins*, meaning daily choices to do the opposite of what God would want. Our sins are like symptoms of our bigger disease—sin.

STEP — MOVING OUT

This step challenges students to remove one roadblock that keeps them from praying.

Option 1  Light the Fire

You'll need Several Bibles to give away; the seven roadblock signs from step 3, option 1; a 2x2-foot poster board; masking or transparent tape; several felt-tip pens and a trash can.

Ahead of time, Create a new roadblock sign from the poster board, shaped like a stop sign with the phrase "Don't Know Jesus Yet" on it. Tape all eight roadblock signs around the meeting area.

Explain: **We've already talked about seven obstacles to prayer. There is another important one: "Don't Know Jesus Yet." I'd like you to come to the front of the room and, with a felt-tip pen, write your name on the sign that is your biggest roadblock to prayer. You can choose more than one. If you're not comfortable coming to the front of the room, you can just sit in your seat and think about what sign(s) apply to you.**

Play some worship music as students write their names. After they have finished, invite students who wrote their names (or would have if they had come up to the front) on the "Don't Know Jesus Yet" sign and would like to know Him to meet with you after the service.

Take the signs down and rip them into small pieces (you can ask some students to help you with this), throw them away in the trash can and close in prayer asking God to help us overcome our roadblocks.

Immediately following the session, call over the students who wrote on the "Don't Know Jesus Yet" sign and huddle up with them. Explain: **You can know Jesus right now if you admit that you've sinned, just like we talked about today, and would like to have a relationship with God. This relationship can only happen if you commit your life to Jesus and ask Him to take control over it.** Lead them through a prayer in which they have the chance to commit their lives to Jesus.

> **Note:** The first study of this Pulse series, *Christianity: The Basics,* has a reproducible handout on pages 95-96 to help guide a student through the steps of accepting Jesus as Savior.

Make sure to have extra Bibles ready to give to any of these students who don't have their own. Get their names and addresses and contact them this week, letting them

Option 2  Fired Up

know how glad you are that they've decided to follow Christ.
You'll need 3x5-inch index cards, pens or pencils and a box (or basket).

Have students share their toughest roadblocks to prayer with the whole group. Hand out an index card and a pen or pencil to each student. Instruct them to write their names and one of their roadblocks on the cards. Put the cards in a box (or basket) and have each student pick a card. If a student gets his own, he should put it back and choose another one. Instruct them to put their cards away and not tell anyone whose card they chose. Challenge students to keep their cards in a place where they will be seen every day (i.e., in their notebook or Bible, on their mirror or nightstand, etc.) and to pray for this person and his or

Option 3  Spread the Fire

her roadblock at least once a day for the coming week.
You'll need The seven roadblocks signs from Step 3, Option 1 and masking or transparent tape.

Tape the signs to various walls and corners around the meeting room and then explain that the same roadblocks that keep us from praying also keep our friends who don't know God from seeking Him. Ask students to think of one of their friends who doesn't know Jesus as Savior yet, then ask them to stand near the roadblock sign that best describes the major reason that their friends are still distant from God. Ask the students gathered around each sign to pray for one anothers' friends, asking God to break through that obstacle that keeps their friends distant from Him. Close by asking students to take the Stop Sign Challenge for this week. Any time they see a stop sign, whether they're walking, biking, skateboarding or riding in a car with someone else, they should pray (with eyes open!) for the person they wrote on the roadblock sign, asking God to draw that person to know Him as Savior, and even use them in the process!

It's Tough to Pray

I think it's hardest to pray when...

The last time I prayed was...

I pray best when...

Sometimes I feel guilty about prayer.

☐ yes   ☐ no

Why?

Roadblocks are things that get in our way. What would you say is the biggest roadblock that keeps you from praying?

I think it's hardest to pray when...

The last time I prayed was...

I pray best when...

Sometimes I feel guilty about prayer.

☐ yes   ☐ no

Why?

Roadblocks are things that get in our way. What would you say is the biggest roadblock that keeps you from praying?

Pulse

The Match Game

Find another person who is your match because he or she has…

The same color shirt as you

The same type of shoes as you

The same color eyes as you

The same number of brothers and sisters

The same age

The same number of pets

The same length of hair

The same favorite type of donut

The same number of toes

The same first period teacher

The same favorite radio station

The same number of letters in their first name as you

Devotions in Motion

WEEK TWO: ROADBLOCKS HINDER OUR PRAYERS

CAUTION FLASH FLOOD AREA

DAY 1

QUICK QUESTIONS

Don't stop now. Head to Matthew 17:14-20.

God Says

Think of the tallest mountain you have ever seen. Hopefully, it's not the mountain of clothes on your bedroom floor! How many bulldozers and dump trucks do you think it would take to move it?

If you have faith the size of a mustard seed (about the size of this dot: ●), the answer to the question above is zero. Faith is believing that God will work. Why is this important when you pray? God might not clean up your room if you ask Him to, but the important thing is to know that He could.

So if you asked God for a new bike and you believe He will give you one, will you wake up and find a new bike in your garage? Why?

I Do

What is a mountain in your life that you need God to move for you? Ask Him now.

DAY 4

FAST FACTS

Head toward the front of the Old Testament and see what 2 Chronicles 7:14 has to say about the best attitude about prayer.

God Says

As Billy thought about the past week, he was feeling pretty good about himself. After all, he didn't lie as much as his friends did. Even when his science partner was cheating on yesterday's test, he didn't. He asked Jesus to be his Savior in camp in third grade, and since then he'd gone to church at least three times a month. Plus he cleaned his room last week before his mom even asked him to. So now when his Sunday School teacher asked Billy and the rest of the class to name any sins they had committed in the last week, Billy's mind went blank.

I Do

Once we ask Jesus to take over our lives, we still continue to sin. That means that we need to keep asking God to forgive us for what we've done. Today take a few minutes to pray humbly and ask God for forgiveness for some of the sins that you've committed this past week.

Pulse

FAST FACTS

To find out how to have the right motives in prayer, check out James 4:3.

God Says

Today Blanca is having a longer prayer time than she usually does. That's because she has more requests than she usually does. She's asking God for a nicer younger brother, a new and improved stereo and all A's on her next report card, even when she doesn't do her homework.

What's wrong with what Blanca is doing? Well, it's pretty simple. She's asking God for selfish things with wrong motives. Instead of praying like Blanca, the right motive in prayer is to ask God for His will to be done.

I Do

What is one thing that you think is probably God's will for you that you can ask Him about right now?

FOLD HERE --

QUICK QUESTIONS

To find out more about the best attitude in prayer, read James 1:5–8.

God Says

What would be the strangest exhibit you could see at a freak show at a state fair?

☐ A man whose arms are eight feet long;

☐ A woman with a full beard and mustache;

☐ A teenager with two minds.

James 1:5–8 talks about a double-minded man. Why is being double minded a problem when we pray?

I Do

Take a few minutes to ask God to help you be single-minded in your prayer life.

42

 **Pulse** Prayer

The Big Idea

Praying is much more than just asking God for help.

Session Aims

In this session you will guide students to:

- Understand the four essential parts of the Lord's prayer;
- Sense God's presence with them as they talk to Him in prayer;
- Learn to pray using the ACTS pattern in their personal prayer times.

The Biggest Verse

"This, then, is how you should pray:
'Our Father in heaven, hallowed be your name,
'Your kingdom come, your will be done on earth as it is in heaven.
'Give us today our daily bread.
'Forgive us our debts, as we also have forgiven our debtors.
'And lead us not into temptation, but deliver us from the evil one.'"
Matthew 6:9-13

Other Important Verses

Matthew 6:5-15; 1 Thessalonians 5:16-18

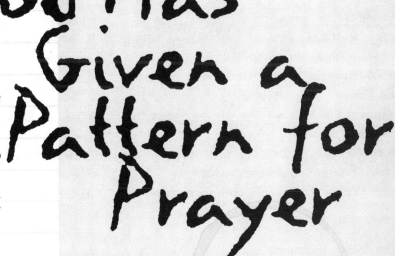

God Has Given a Pattern for Prayer

STEP

MOVING IN

This step introduces the idea that our prayers are often very shallow and self-centered.

Option 1 — Move It

You'll need Four pieces of paper for signs, a felt-tip pen and masking or transparent tape.

Ahead of time, write the words "Yes," "Never," "Sometimes" and "Clueless" on four pieces of paper and tape them to the four corners or walls of the room.

Greet students and ask them all to stand in the middle of the room. Point out the taped signs and explain that when you read one of the following prayer facts, students should move to the corner of the room that best fits them. Read the following list slowly, allowing students time to move to their corners:

My family prays before meals.

I pray at least once a day.

I pray at really strange moments.

The only time I pray is before stressful things like tests.

I pray before I go to sleep.

The only prayer I know is the one that starts "Now I lay me down to sleep."

The only prayer I know is the one that says "Good grub, good meat, good God, let's eat."

It's OK to pray that your favorite sports team wins the game.

Prayer should be allowed in schools.

Prayer should be mandatory for one minute at the start of every school day.

I prayed at my school's flagpole on "See You at the Pole" day.

My family has intense prayer sessions together.

I sometimes feel like I don't know what to say when I'm supposed to pray.

I'm praying right now that this activity will end shortly.

Instruct everyone to return to their seats and let them know that their last prayer was answered! Discuss:

Were you surprised by how many people went to one corner on any of the questions?

Which question was the toughest for you to answer?

Were there any questions that made you uncomfortable? Why?

Explain: **Most of us have pretty empty or shallow prayer times in which we ask for things we want or make general statements such as "Thank you, God for this day; help me pass my science test and bless my family and friends." Very few people pray beyond the occasional prayer at meals. We're going to try to change that in this session. We want to make prayer a deeper conversation with God, but still make it enjoyable and easy to do.**

Option 2 — Chat Room

You'll need A TV, a VCR and the video *Apollo 13.*

Ahead of time, cue the video approximately one hour 56 minutes from the opening Universal graphic to the scene that talks about the prayers offered around the world for the astronauts in the crippled Apollo 13 spaceship.

After viewing the video clip, discuss the following:

Do you think that most of the people who pray during a big crisis pray at other times as well? Why or why not?

Sometimes the people who pray during a crisis are the same folks who never give God a moment during good times. Do you think God listens to their prayers anyway? Why or why not?

Have you ever prayed during a world crisis? What happened as a result of your prayer?

When do you usually pray?

Do you think your prayers are pretty basic, praying mostly at meals and at bedtime?

Explain: **Today we're going to see prayer as communication between us and God that is much deeper than just asking for help or thanking Him for food.**

NOTES

Option 3  Fun and Games

You'll need Four copies of "The Word Game" sheet (pp. 51-52) cut into four pieces, each containing a definition.

Ask for the smartest people in the room to raise their hands. Select four volunteers and bring them to the front of the room. Tell them they're going to play a version of "Balderdash", a game of zany word definitions.

Give each volunteer one of the cut-out slips of paper. Explain that one of them has the true definition of the word and the other three have false definitions. Send them out of the room for three minutes to work on their definitions. When they come back, their goal is to try and read their definition in such a way that they convince the group that their definition is the correct one. While you're waiting for the volunteers to return, sing a praise song or two!

When all four volunteers have finished reading their definitions, have the rest of the group vote for the definition that they think is correct, then reveal the correct one. If the students are pretty clever, let them create their own false definition to make it more fun. **Note:** There are enough words on the sheet for three rounds. You can create more with a thesaurus and a dictionary.

When the game is over, explain: **All of these words have to do with communication and/or prayer. Unfortunately, most of us don't know much about words like that because our own prayers are nothing more than asking God for help when we're desperate. But we're going to change that today, and don't worry, we'll use simpler words than "auscultation" and "interlocution."**

STEP 2 — MOVING UP

This step helps students understand the relevance of the Lord's Prayer to their own lives.

Option 1  Move It

You'll need Your Bible and three copies of "If God Talked Back" (pp. 53-54). **Option:** A sound system with one microphone set up on stage and one in the back of the room.

Ahead of time, choose a student to be the "stage" character and find someone with a fairly deep voice (sixth-grade, prepubescent boys are not recommended for this role) to play the "voice." Give each actor a copy of "If God Talked Back."

Ask for a student volunteer to read Matthew 6:9-13. Explain: **Many of us have heard that prayer several times. It's probably the most famous prayer in the world but it's become so routine that we don't think about what it really means anymore.**

Ask the two actors to read the script, with the stage character in plain view and the voice character hidden. After the dramatization, discuss: **How was what the "voice" said different from what you expected? How does this make you think differently about this famous prayer?**

Option 2  Chat Room

You'll need Several Bible translations, copies of "The Lord's Prayer" (p. 55) and pens or pencils.

Have several volunteers read the Lord's Prayer from Matthew 6:9-13 from the different Bible versions. Before they read, mention to students that the Lord's Prayer might sound different from the way they remember it.

Divide students into groups of two or three and distribute copies of "The Lord's Prayer" and pens or pencils. Give them a few minutes to complete them, then bring the group together and discuss their answers. Ask:

Why do you think Jesus prays to "our" Father? To stress that God isn't just His Father, but the Father to all who know Him.

If God's already holy, then why are we praying that God's name be "hallowed" or "holy"? We aren't praying that God may become holy, but that He may be treated as holy.

What is God's kingdom? That which has been brought under God's sovereignty and serves Him as King.

What does "bread" mean? Not just our need for bread but our need for food in general, and beyond that our physical needs for health and a place to live.

Why is it "daily" bread? So that the disciples will learn to rely on Jesus every day and know that every bit of food and physical aid comes from God each day.

What are the "debts" that we ask God to forgive? Does that mean our parents' credit card bills or something? No, it means the things we do against God, which in this case is our sin against Him.

Explain: **The prayer Jesus gave us is really a pattern for prayer; we're going to look at the parts of that pattern next.**

Option 3  Pulse Points

You'll need A backpack, a blank name tag, a felt-tip pen, a calendar, a loaf of bread, a chain and a map.

Ahead of time, place all of the above items in the backpack. In addition, you may want to tape a piece of paper to your backpack that says "Lord's Prayer Backpack."

Share the following true story:

About 50 years ago a Jewish doctor in Russia named Boris Kornfeld was sent to a concentration camp in Siberia. His life there was terrible, though it was probably a little better than most because he was a doctor and could help the guards as well as the prisoners. He was bitter for several years because of his imprisonment, knowing that he was unjustly accused of the crime. During his

time in prison he came to know another prisoner who was a Christian. Boris was not interested in Christians, but this particular man was unique: instead of being bitter about his imprisonment, he talked about how everybody deserves some form of punishment but that God in Christ could help. He continually recited the Lord's Prayer until Boris also knew it by heart.

One day the other prisoner was sent away, but Boris could not stop thinking about the Lord's Prayer. It was in his head night and day. The truth of Christ finally got through, and Boris decided to become a Christian. It changed his whole way of thinking, even to the point that he knew he had to stand up against certain things that happened in the prison that he had gone along with before. Once he made these stands, he knew his life would soon be over because he was making too many people angry.

Boris wanted to tell somebody of his decision to follow Christ. One night he had another prisoner in his medical care who was seriously ill and he took the opportunity to tell this other man about his conversion to Christ. The next morning the patient asked to talk to his new doctor friend but was told that Boris had been murdered the night before. Just like Boris, this man could not stop thinking about what he had been told about Jesus Christ. Soon he too became a Christian!

Now here's the really cool part of the story: this man was Aleksandr Solzhenitsyn, who went on to become a great Russian writer and a strong Christian. He even won the Nobel prize for writing (one of the best awards in the world) and has become one of the most influential Christian writers of the twentieth century. All because someone shared the Lord's Prayer with Boris Kornfeld who in turn shared the story of Christ with Aleksandr Solzhenitsyn.

Explain: **You may be wondering about this Lord's Prayer that is so powerful in this story. Well, I'll read it to you.** Read Matthew 6:9-13 aloud. Ask: **How many of you have heard this prayer before? How many of you can even say this prayer aloud?** Depending on how well churched your students are and how liturgical your church is, you will probably have several students who have at least heard this prayer and some who can even say it aloud.

Continue: **The words in this prayer are 2,000 years old and yet they are still super-powerful. This prayer is powerful because of five really important things it teaches us to ask God about that we're going to study right now.**

1. His Perfection

Point out the phrase, **"Our Father in heaven, hallowed be your name."** Explain: **Hallowed means "holy or per- fect." This doesn't mean that our prayers make God holy. He is already holy and perfect. We just pray that people recognize Him as such.** Call attention to the backpack and remove the name tag, explaining: **If God were to wear a name tag, one thing we learn from this prayer is that He would be called holy.** Write the word "Perfection" on the name tag and place it on one of your student's shoulders, making sure to clarify that it's GOD who is perfect, not the student.

2. His Will

Begin: **Now let's look at the next verse, "Your kingdom come, your will be done on earth as it is in heaven."** Remove the calendar from your backpack and explain: **Asking for God's will to be done means submitting your whole life, including your time and everything you do each day, to His plan for you.**

3. His Food

Even though God is holy and powerful, He still is involved in meeting our daily needs. Remove the loaf of bread from the backpack as you explain: **We are to remember that God gives us our food every day. Sure, He supplies it through our parents, a restaurant or the store, but He is ultimately the one who provides our food.**

4. His Forgiveness

Explain: **We owe a big debt to God and that's why we are supposed to pray that God would "forgive us our debts."** But this debt isn't a Visa card. No, it's the debt of our sin. At this point, take out the chain and place it around your neck as you continue: **God sent His son, Jesus Christ, as payment for our sin. That allows us to know Him personally, and empowers us to forgive other people as Jesus prays, "as we also have forgiven our debtors."** You can remove the chain from your neck as you explain about the forgiveness that comes through Jesus.

God Has Given a Pattern for Prayer

47

5. His Protection

Begin: **There is an evil one who is looking to destroy us. His name is Satan, and we need God to help us.** Remove the map from the backpack and conclude: ~~Just like this map tells us where to go~~, we should ask God to show us ~~where to go~~ *how* to stay away from tempting situations at school or home that might cause us to turn from what God wants us to do. If you have time, you might want to mention specific tempting situations, such as being tempted to cheat on homework because you want to watch your favorite TV show, lie to your parent about what you did yesterday with a friend because you don't want to be grounded, or gossip to impress a new friend.

STEP 3 — MOVING ON

This step teaches students the ACTS pattern of prayer.

Option 1 — Chat Room

You'll need Tape or tacks and four large sheets of poster board, each with one letter of the ACTS pattern written on it with the corresponding word it represents.

Ahead of time, make signs using the poster board by writing each of the following letters and corresponding words from the ACTS pattern on a separate sheet: A for Adoration, C for Confession, T for Thanksgiving, and S for Supplication). Tape or tack the signs to the ceiling of the meeting room before the session.

Explain: **If you've tried to pray, maybe you've gotten stuck because you don't know what to pray about. You mention a few requests, like your history test and your aunt's back surgery but that's about it. Today you're going to learn another pattern for prayer that will help you get past boring and superficial prayers. In fact, it resembles "The Lord's Prayer" in several ways.**

A **for Adoration: Praising God for who He is, as Jesus does in the Lord's Prayer by saying, "Hallowed be your name."** Ask students to call out some things about God that define who He is, such as loving, awesome, all-powerful.

C **for Confession: Admitting the bad things that we have done, as Jesus does in the Lord's Prayer by modeling, "Forgive us."** Ask students to brainstorm some of the sins they might need to confess to God such as cheating, lying, laziness, talking back to parents, gossip, etc.

T **for Thanksgiving: Telling God thanks for what He has done.** Have students call out things in their lives that they are thankful for.

S **for Supplication: Asking God to help us and others with problems and needs.** Have students call out things they need help with as modeled in the Lord's Prayer, " Give us today our daily bread," "And lead us not into temptation."

When you're done, say **Amen** and ask students to return to their seats. Conclude: **We have just said a very creative prayer to God together by using the pattern He gave us to pray. Now, try to remember this pattern and use it this week when you're by yourselves.**

Option 2 — Real Life

Note: You will need to teach the ACTS pattern from Option 1: Chat Room at the end of this step so use Option 2 in addition to Option 1 if you have time, but *not in place of it.*

You'll need Just this book!

Ahead of time, practice telling the following story in your own words.

Explain: **Maybe you can relate to a seventh grader I heard about named Kasey.**

Kasey had lots of friends at school and even got in trouble at times for talking with them during class, especially Mr. Fong's Math class. As soon as Kasey got home, she picked up the phone and talked to her friends for several more hours about everything ranging from the cute new guy who had just started at the school to the new black sweater that she wanted. She talked so much that soon her mom had to put her on phone restriction just so she'd get her homework done.

One Tuesday while Kasey was on phone restriction, she figured she'd try this prayer thing that she had been learning about at church. So she sat down and prayed for everything she could think

of: her uncle's need for a job, her best friend who had a cold and had missed school that day and her neighbor across the street who didn't go to church. This took all of about three minutes.

Instead of feeling excited that she had prayed, Kasey felt a little sad. She had heard that prayer was supposed to be so great, and here it felt like she just said a few "give me" sentences to God and that was about it. She figured there had to be more but just didn't know what more to do while she prayed.

Ask students: **Have you ever felt like Kasey, like there was more to praying than just a few "give me" sentences before you went to bed? Today we're going to learn a way to have a prayer adventure with God at any time. Sure, it will take more time than three minutes, but I don't think you'll be sorry.**

Return to Option 1 and briefly explain the ACTS pattern for prayer.

Option 3 — Tough Questions

Note: You will need to teach the ACTS pattern from Option 1: Chat Room for prayer at the end of this step so use Option 1 in addition to this option if you have time, but *not in place of it*.

You'll need Just the following questions. Use them in small groups by writing them on the board, an overhead transparency or on sheets of paper.

Divide students into small groups and discuss the following:

1. **Why should we pray for God to not lead us into temptation? Would God ever lead us this way?** This puzzling statement is probably a figure of speech where something is negated by expressing the opposite. "Lead us not into it, but away from it."

2. Read Matthew 6:8. **If God knows what we need before we ask Him, like Jesus says in Matthew 6:8, why do we have to pray?** Since God is all knowing, of course He knows everything that we need. But the purpose of prayer is not getting what we want from God; it's building a relationship with Him. It's our relationship with Him that motivates us to pray, not our selfish desire to get stuff from Him.

3. **Why do we pray that God's will be done? If God is so strong, can anything stop His will?** Well, lots of people have disagreed about the extent of God's sovereignty over the last few centuries. Although God is all powerful, it is possible that our sin, or even the evil one mentioned in Matthew 6:13, can thwart His will from being done.

4. **Does "forgive us our debts, as we also have forgiven our debtors" mean that God will only forgive us if we forgive other people?** Good question, but the answer is no. God forgives us when we ask Him to. Yet the point of the verse is that our lifestyle should be permeated with forgiveness, meaning we not only ask God for forgiveness but we are quick to forgive others when they do something wrong to us.

We've looked at a lot of aspects of the Lord's Prayer and the pattern to pray. Let's see if we can put it into practice. At this point, transition back to Option 1: Chat Room and briefly explain the ACTS prayer pattern.

NOTES

STEP 4

MOVING OUT

This step challenges students to commit to praying the ACTS pattern this week during their personal prayer times.

Before You Begin an Option

All three options in this step begin with the following activity:

Ask a student to read 1 Thessalonians 5:16-18. Discuss: **How can a person possibly pray all the time?** The answer is by maintaining an attitude of prayer, talking to God at all moments instead of just when you sit down to pray.

Ask another student to read Matthew 6:5-7 and then ask: **What does this say about how we should pray or about our attitudes when we pray?** When Jesus commands us not to "babble" in our prayers in Matthew 6:7, He's not condemning long prayers. He is condemning a common prayer practice in His day of using long lists of names of multiple gods, hoping that the constant and repetitious naming of various gods would bring greater results. Jesus is condemning long prayers only if they are meaningless, not if they are meaningful. The point is to pray in public without making a big deal about it; not praying in front of others to show off or to show how spiritual you are, but to be more concerned about communicating with God.

Option 1  Light the Fire

You'll need Several permanent ink felt-tip pens.

Distribute felt-tip pens and have students write ACTS on their palms. Before the ink washes away (within a day probably given the way junior highers' hands tend to sweat) tell them that every time they look at the letters on their hand to quickly pray through the pattern. They could make a quick comment to God about how great He is, confess sins they have done, thank God for something He has done, and ask for help with a problem.

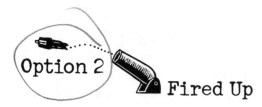

Option 2 Fired Up

You'll need Copies of "The ACTS Calendar" (p. 56) and pens or pencils.

Distribute "The ACTS Calendar" to each student and explain that for each day of the week, they should write something for adoration, confession, thanksgiving and supplication. Give them time to write in today's boxes right now.

Option 3  Spread the Fire

You'll need Felt-tip pens, brightly colored paper and tape.

Ahead of time, make four signs that read, "Adoration," "Confession," "Thanksgiving" and "Supplication." Also, ask four responsible students or adult leaders to be prepared to lead one of the following discussion groups: Adoration, Confession, Thanksgiving and Supplication. Tape the signs to the four corners of the room.

Explain: **Not only is ACTS a great pattern for prayer, it's also a way we can tell others about Jesus.** Divide students into four smaller groups and send each group to one of the room's corners with one of the leaders chosen in advance.

Explain that each group should brainstorm ways that they could share about Jesus with others through the topic assigned to their corner. For example, those in the Adoration corner might mention that the next time they see a brilliant sunset with a friend, they could say something cool about God Who made it. Or the Confession corner might realize that the next time they do something wrong, they could share with a non-Christian friend how bad they feel when they sin and how much they need Jesus' forgiveness.

Have each group spend three minutes on the first topic, then ask the leaders to take the assigned signs and move to another small group. Have the leaders continue to move from group to group until all four groups have discussed how to witness using each point.

The Word Game

Interlocution:

Interchange of speech; dialogue; an intermediate act or degree before the final decision. (You have the correct definition!)

Interlocution:

The process of routing railroad trains to their appropriate destinations.

Interlocution:

The degree of voltage used in an electrical circuit, primarily in circuit board applications.

Interlocution:

An unusual act or government decree whereby an elected representative is allowed to make contrary statements to a budget proposal.

Supplication:

Exceedingly humble and earnest prayer; a plea given in a humble manner. (You have the correct definition!)

Supplication:

The preparation of an evening meal, used primarily in the mountainous regions of Scotland.

Supplication:

Affecting the mind with a sense of appreciation for the outdoors.

Supplication:

Supplication: The cutting open of insects for study and scientific research.

Auscultation:

Auscultation: A method of listening, primarily for the purpose of discovering a disease. (You have the correct definition!)

Auscultation:

Auscultation: The process of debate by one or more members of a cultic group.

Auscultation:

Auscultation: A system of measurements used in cooking pursuits.

Auscultation:

Auscultation: The unusual and strange dance that certain members of the canine family exhibit when chasing after their posteriors.

Needed: two microphones, one set up on stage and one off-stage.

If God Talked Back

Stage: "Our Father, which art in heaven..."[1]

Voice: Yes?

Stage: Who's that?

Voice: It's God. You called?

Stage: No, I didn't.

Voice: You said "Our Father."

Stage: Yeah, but I didn't mean anything by it.

Voice: Well, you got My attention. Go on.

Stage: Sure. "Hallowed be thy name."

Voice: What does that mean?

Stage: How should I know? It's in the prayer.

Voice: If you're going to pray it, you should know what it means.

Stage: I guess so. What does it mean?

Voice: Holy--My name is holy!

Stage: Okay, okay. I'll remember next time. Can I go on now? I don't have all day.

Voice: If you want to.

Stage: "Thy kingdom come."

Voice: Whoa!

Stage: What now?

Voice: Do you really want My kingdom to come?

Stage: I don't know. I never thought about it before.

Voice: Well, think about it.

Stage: Yeah, I guess so. Having Your kingdom here would be pretty cool, I guess.

Voice: It will be awesome. Keep going.

Stage: "Thy will be done, on earth as it is in heaven." (pause) Well?

Voice: Well what?

Stage: Well, aren't You going to interrupt me again?

Voice: Do you really want My will done?

Stage: Sure. That's up to You, not me.

Voice: No, it's up to you to obey My will.

Stage: Oh, I hadn't thought of that. "Give us this day our daily bread."

Voice: You could use a little less bread.

Stage: Don't remind me.

Voice: And you could stand to be a little more thankful for the food you eat each day. That cute little prayer you like to say: "Good grub, good meat, good God, let's eat" is pretty cheesy.

Stage: It's quick, and I'm always hungry.

Voice: Like I said, you could stand to cut out some of the bread, not to mention the jelly donuts.

Stage: I guess You're right. "And forgive us our debts...." Hey! I could use my debts forgiven. My VISA card is maxed.

Voice: Not those debts--your sins. If you ask, I'll forgive them.

Prayer

Stage: Okay, uhhh uhhh   Please forgive me for how I treated my mom yesterday?

Voice: Done. Keep going.

Stage: "As we forgive our debtors." That doesn't seem too bad. I forgive my Dad for hogging the TV last night, Grandma for the socks she gave me for Christmas.

Voice: What about Julie?

Stage: Why'd You have to bring that up? Apparently, You don't understand what she did to me. She was downright mean to me last week.

Voice: But I do understand completely. You need to forgive her.

Stage: If I forgive her, then I can't bring it up at our next argument.

Voice: I won't bring up the four zillion things you've done either.

Stage: Good point. Can I finish now?

Voice: Please do.

Stage: (*long pause*) Amen.

Voice: Oops, not quite. Finish it up right.

Stage: Can't.

Voice: Why not?

Stage: I know what You're going to say.

Voice: About what?

Stage: About my temptations.

Voice: You're catching on. Go on, pray it.

Stage: Oh boy. "And lead us not into temptation..."

Voice: I'd be happy to, but you've got to do your part too—like staying off those disgusting web pages.

Stage: I knew You'd bring that up. But it's so hard to stop.

Voice: That's why you have Me. I can help. Really.

Stage: I know. I guess I do need Your help. Please keep me from temptation.

Voice: I'll be there.

Stage: I feel like Satan's out to get me. Can You help keep him from me?

Voice: Yes.

Stage: I feel better already.

Voice: Why don't you wrap up the prayer with a big finish.

Stage: You bet. "For thine is the kingdom, and the power, and the glory, for ever.

Voice: (*buzzer noise*) Try again.

Stage: (*A little louder*) "For thine is the kingdom, and the power, and the glory, for ever."

Voice: Come on, it's a big finish. Say it like you mean it. LET ME HEAR IT!

Stage: "FOR THINE IS THE KINGDOM, AND THE POWER, AND THE GLORY, FOR EVER! AMEN!"

Voice: Well done.

Stage: Can I go know?

Voice: Sure. But I hope to see you tomorrow, and I hope you'll think about what you're praying next time instead of just parroting the words.

Stage: Got it. Uhhh, thanks, God. See You tomorrow.

Note:

1. Direct quotes are taken from *King James Version*.

The Lord's Prayer

Have you heard the Lord's Prayer before? ❑ yes ❑ no

Do you know it by heart? ❑ yes ❑ no

Next to each phrase, write what you think it means.

Our Father in heaven

Hallowed be your name

Your kingdom come

Your will be done

On earth as it is in heaven

Give us today our daily bread

Forgive us our debts

As we also have forgiven our debtors

Lead us not into temptation

But deliver us from the evil one

The ACTS Calendar

Each day this week, write something to fill the Adoration, Confession, Thanksgiving and Supplication columns. Be creative! Come up with something new each day.

	A	C	T	S
Sunday				
Monday				
Tuesday				
Wednesday				
Thursday				
Friday				
Saturday				

Devotions in Motion

WEEK THREE: GOD HAS GIVEN A PATTERN FOR PRAYER

DAY 1

FAST FACTS

Quick! Flip open your Bible to Psalm 9:1,2 and see what God has to say about adoring Him in prayer.

God Says

You stumble out of bed and head down the hall to the bathroom to take a shower and get ready for school. Just as you're turning the knob on the bathroom door, your mom stops you and without saying hello, bursts into a long list of things she needs you to do today: "Make sure you take the lunch money I left out for you on the counter. Plus tell your teacher that I'll be 15 minutes late for the parent/teacher conference today. After school, I need you to empty the dishwasher and make sure your little brother does his homework."

That's not a very pleasant way to say "good morning" to you, is it? And yet that's what we do to God when we begin all of our prayers by diving right into our list of things we want Him to do.

I Do

Before you ask God to do anything for you today, write out seven things about God that you really appreciate as a time of adoration.

FOLD HERE

DAY 4

QUICK QUESTIONS

Don't waste any more time but head to Psalm 59:1 –5.

God Says

What is the best summary of the attitude of the writer of this psalm?

☐ I can either ask a friend to help me or I can ask God.

☐ If I think about it long enough, I'll come up with my own plan.

☐ God is the only One who can help me.

In the midst of asking God for help, how does the writer continue to adore God in Psalm 59:5?

I Do

What are three things you know you need God's help for? Take a few minutes to pray about all three things.

Even as you pray, how can you continue to adore God for how cool He is?

QUICK QUESTIONS

If you're wondering what to do when you've done something wrong and don't know how to pray about it, turn to Psalm 51:1-12.

God Says

Let's define sin as falling short of what God would want us to do. How does the author of this psalm, David, feel about his sin?

☐ Really bad because he knows it's wrong;

☐ Really bad because he got caught;

☐ OK about his sin because he's human after all

How long has David been a sinner?

☐ Since he was born;

☐ Since he was eight years old and ate a stale pizza;

☐ Since he turned 12 and puberty caused his voice to change.

According to David in Psalm 51:12, what is the end result of asking God to forgive his sin?

I Do

Choose one of these three areas—your family, your friends or school—and think of a few sins you've committed recently in that area. Take three minutes to confess them to God and ask Him to forgive you and blot out those sins.

FOLD HERE

FAST FACTS

To find out what to do the next time you feel somewhat "blah," read Psalm 100:1-5.

God Says

It's 5:30 p.m. on Wednesday and Rebecca is getting bored. Right after school she came home to do her homework, and although her history report on John Quincy Adams was hard, it wasn't as bad as she thought it was going to be. But now there's nothing much to eat in the refrigerator except a bunch of fruit. And the only thing she can find on television is a diet infomercial.

Think hard and try to find at least five things that Rebecca can thank God for that she's not appreciating. There's no cure for boredom and the "blahs" like thanking God in prayer.

I Do

We often spend more time whining to God about our problems than thanking Him for everything that He's already done. Take your age and think of that many things to thank God for. For example, if you're 13, think of 13 things to thank God for.

Pulse Prayer

The Big Idea

Since prayer has many forms, we can talk to God in all sorts of different ways.

Session Aims

In this session you will guide students to:

* Discover and learn a variety of methods and types of prayer;
* Experience the power of prayer and God's presence together with others in the youth ministry;
* Respond by praying the words of Scripture.

The Biggest Verse

"Pray in the Spirit on all occasions with all kinds of prayers and requests. With this in mind, be alert and always keep on praying for all the saints."
Ephesians 6:18

Other Important Verses

Psalm 22:1-8,14-21; 32:6,7; 139:4; Isaiah 6:1-8; Daniel 6:10; Jonah 2:1; Matthew 6:5,6; 26:39; Mark 15:21-39; Acts 6:6; 1 Timothy 2:8; James 5:13,14

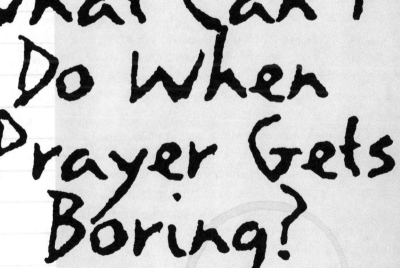

What Can I Do When Prayer Gets Boring?

STEP 1 MOVING IN

This step reminds students that communication between people comes in many diverse forms.

Option 1 Move It

You'll need Paper, pens or pencils and a candy prize.

Ahead of time, meet with two of your most expressive (maybe even obnoxious) students, adult leaders or parents. Divide the following list of communication methods evenly between them: smoke signals, singing, writing a letter, yelling, facial expressions, body language, car radio, Morse code, E-mail, talking, sign language, telephone, CB radio and an answering machine. Have the volunteers practice an approximately three- to five-second demonstration of each of their modes of communication before the meeting. They may use words, but they should try to use them sparingly. Facial expressions, hand motions and body language should be the main clues.

Greet students and explain that you've got two friends who will be acting out some very important things. Challenge students to remember everything the actors act out because the student who remembers the most will receive a prize.

Ask the two volunteers to come to the front of the room. The first one should start with a three- to five-second demonstration of one of their methods of communication. Then that person freezes and the second one does a demonstration for three to five seconds, then freezes. At this point, the first person unfreezes and acts out a third mode of communication. This continues until the entire list of communication methods has been demonstrated.

Thank the two actors for their Oscar-award-winning performances and distribute paper and a pen or pencil to each student. Allow two minutes to write down as many forms of communication that they can remember. Give a prize to the student who remembers the most.

Ask: **What did all of these have in common? As we've seen today, communication comes in a lot of forms. Today we're going to take a look at how we can use some of these forms in our communication with God through prayer.**

Option 2 Chat Room

You'll need Trash bags, magazines, newspapers, scissors and masking or transparent tape.

Greet students, then divide them into two teams: boys vs. girls. **Note:** If you have more than 20 students, you may want to have more than one girls team and more than one boys team. Explain: **Today we're going to see who is better at communication: the boys or the girls.** Lay all of the magazines and newspapers out on the floor and explain that the teams are to find pictures that show ways that we can communicate with each other. Share that the key is to be creative and look for pictures of people singing, yelling, dancing, making weird faces, whatever. Explain that each team needs to appoint a picture collector who will be collecting them in an unusual way. This person is going to put the garbage bag over his or her head. Each teammate is going to tape the pictures to the bag while the "collector" is wearing it.

> **Note:** Make your church's insurance agent happy by cutting a hole in the garbage bag first!

After five to seven minutes of cutting pictures and taping them onto the bags, bring the students wearing the bags to the front of the room and comment on the variety of pictures they are wearing. Transition to the rest of the lesson by explaining: **There are so many ways to communicate with each other. Not only that; there are a ton of ways to communicate with God. We're going to look at some of these for the next few minutes.** Discuss:

Other than talking, what are ways you can communicate to others how you are feeling? Laughing, dancing, body gestures, smiling, crying, etc.

Other than talking, what are ways you can communicate to God how you are feeling? Singing, dancing, silent meditation on His Word, etc.

Prayer to God can be much more than merely a few words before you go to sleep. Where's the most unusual place you've ever prayed? You might want to share some of your own stories at this point to stimulate conversation, like the time you bungee-jumped off the Grand Canyon.

God knows what we will say even before we say it (see Psalm 139:4). **What does this tell you about your communication with Him?** He can understand your deepest thoughts and feelings even when you don't express them well verbally.

Can you think of different ways in which God communicates with us? Through His Word, His Spirit, His creation, other people, etc.

Option 3 — Fun and Games

You'll need: Eight 3x5-inch index cards, a container of play dough and a stopwatch.

Ahead of time, write each of the following words on a separate index card: "telephone," "television," "mouth," "pen," "book," "computer," "CD" and "ear."

Greet students and divide them into two teams. Team One chooses a person to go first. When she comes up to the front of the room, show her one of the index cards you prepared. Instruct her to think about the word on the card, then give her the play dough and tell her she must use the play dough to communicate with her team what the object is. Absolutely no words can be used. Time how long it takes for Team One to guess and then ask for a volunteer from Team Two to repeat the process. Continue until all of the objects on the list are used. Congratulate the winning team.

When the game is over, ask: **What do all of these objects have in common?** They are all ways we can communicate with other people. **What are some other ways to communicate with people?**

Continue: **Today we're going to learn about all of the ways we can communicate with God through prayer.**

NOTES

STEP 2 — MOVING UP

This step helps students understand that there are many ways to communicate with God through prayer.

Option 1 — Move It

You'll need Several Bibles, pens or pencils and 3x5-inch index cards.

Ahead of time, write out each of the following Bible verses on separate index cards: Daniel 6:10; Jonah 2:1; Matthew 6:5,6; Matthew 26:39; Acts 6:6; 1 Timothy 2:8; James 5:13,14.

Choose one student to come to the front of the room and pick a verse card. Read the card aloud. Once you're done reading that verse, the student will act out the type or method of prayer that the Bible passage describes. That person gets to choose another student, who will select another card and act out that type or method of prayer. That student gets to choose another student, and so on until the verses have all been acted out.

Here are the verses followed by some possible ideas of what students should be acting out.

Daniel 6:10—Pray on your knees.

Jonah 2:1—Pray anywhere.

Matthew 6:5,6—Pray in private without acting like a big shot.

Matthew 26:39—Pray lying flat on your face.

Acts 6:6—Lay hands on people while you're praying for them.

1 Timothy 2:8—Lift up your hands while you pray.

James 5:13,14—Pray when you're in trouble; when you are happy, pray with songs; when you are sick, have elders anoint you with oil and pray.

Read Ephesians 6:18 aloud, then explain: **God is so creative that He's given us all sorts of ways to pray to Him. Prayer is more than just talking. Just like there are different ways people communicate with each other, there are different ways to communicate with God. In the Bible, a person's body position was often impor-**

tant; sometimes they sang their prayers or prayed in unusual places. Next we're going to learn how we can use Scripture as a creative prayer tool.

Option 2 Chat Room

You'll need Several Bibles, copies of "Tons of Types" (p. 67) and pens or pencils.

Ask for volunteers to read Ephesians 6:18 and 1 Timothy 2:8 aloud. Explain: **In Ephesians, Paul encourages us to explore all different types of prayer and then in 1 Timothy, Paul gives us an example of one way to pray.** Ask for two volunteers to come to the front of the room. Instruct them to lift up both of their arms and to keep them lifted until you tell them to put them down.

Distribute a copy of "Tons of Types" and a pen or pencil to each of the other students. Allow several minutes to complete the handout, then bring everyone together (be sure the two students are keeping their arms raised) and ask: **Which of these seems the strangest to you? Why? Why do you think God would want us to pray in so many different ways?** The answer is that He's a creative God and He has all sorts of ways to communicate with us.

You can now tell the two volunteers to lower their arms. Ask them: **How are your arms feeling? Aren't you glad we can pray in all sorts of ways, not just with our arms lifted up?**

Option 3  Pulse Points

You'll need Several Bibles and a magazine with pictures in it.

Ask: **Did you know it's OK to pray no matter what your circumstances? For example, the best way to pray at school is like this:**

> Just as your teacher is beginning class, stand up on your chair, raise your arms, face toward heaven and shout, "OH LORD! MAKER OF HEAVEN AND EARTH! WE ASK YOU THIS DAY TO INSTRUCT US THROUGH THE MOUTH OF YOUR SERVANT, MR. DETWEILER! AMEN AND AMEN!" Then sit down.

Believe me, your friends and teacher will appreciate your willingness to pray for the class.

OK, so it might not turn out so great. But it's true, you know. You can really pray at all sorts of times. Paul writes about that in Ephesians 6:18. Read the verse aloud and then transition to the three main points:

1. When do we pray? On all occasions.

Illustration: Open the magazine, walk up to a student and randomly flip it open to a picture. Ask that student to think of one thing to pray about in whatever scene the picture is showing. Do this five to eight times until students understand that there are always things to pray about in every occasion.

2. How do we pray? With all kinds of prayers and requests.

Illustration: **Just as we saw in our first activity** (Step 1: Moving In, pp. 60-61) **that we can communicate with each other in all sorts of ways, we can also communicate with God in all sorts of cool ways. Scripture talks about praying in the following ways: by singing, while kneeling, while laying flat on our faces, laying hands on others and lifting up our hands** (see Ephesians 6:18 and 1 Timothy 2:8).

3. For whom do we pray? All the saints.

Illustration: **Saints aren't dead holy people. They are the people who know and follow Jesus.** Ask students to pray for one Christian right then and there. After 20 seconds explain that we can pray for people who know Jesus anytime we think about them.

STEP 3
MOVING ON

This step encourages students to use the actual words of Scripture when they pray.

Option 1 — Chat Room

You'll need Several Bibles and three chairs.

Ahead of time, place the chairs at the front of the meeting room.

Greet students and ask for three volunteers to sit in the three chairs at the front of the room. Explain that they are going to create a continuous prayer together by saying one word at a time, in turn. For example, the first person says a word, such as "Dear"; the second person adds a word, such as "God"; the third person adds another word, such as "we"; then it's the first person's turn again, for instance, adding "thank." The volunteers keep taking turns adding words until the prayer is finished. Although the first few words are easy, it gets more complicated as students have to think of more things to pray about. You can also let audience members volunteer to take the place of someone who is stumped.

Ask: **How many of you have ever started to pray and couldn't think of what to say?** Explain: **It's a common problem. If we don't have some terrible crisis or important decision in our lives, we can't think of what to talk to God about. We find ourselves at a total loss for words.**

Ask students to think of as many well-known prayers or prayer phrases as they can. They'll probably come up with things like "Now I lay me down to sleep" and song versions of meal prayers. After a few have been shared, ask: **Is it okay to use these simple prayers? Does God like these patterns for praying? What's good and what's bad about using prayers like these?**

After a few responses, ask if they've ever been asked to pray in public and didn't know what to say. Share a story where that happened to you, and you found yourself babbling about something meaningless. For example, many adults have had this happen when asked to pray spontaneously in front of the whole church.

Introduce the idea of using the Bible as the actual words of our prayers, called praying through Scripture. Read Ephesians 6:18 again and point out the phrase "pray in the Spirit." Continue: **Since the Bible was inspired through the Holy Spirit, reading its inspired words is one great way to pray in the Spirit. We're going to conclude the session today by creatively praying through a passage from the Old Testament.**

Option 2 — Real Life

You'll need Paper and pens or pencils.

Read the following case study:

John Lee is an eighth-grade guy who has a problem. He's a nice kid, who is active in his church's youth group, and he really desires to have a better relationship with God. In fact, ever since he made a commitment to deepen that relationship at last year's summer camp, he has tried very hard to do the right things to connect himself to God.

But something has gone wrong. It seems like no matter how hard John tries, he can't make his relationship with God real. At the root of the problem is this whole business about praying to God. He keeps telling himself that he needs to pray more, but it just isn't happening. If he tries to pray before breakfast, he finds himself thinking about Fruit Loops. If he tries to pray before class, he finds himself instantly daydreaming about Susan, the girl who sits three rows in front of him. Even at church, when someone starts to pray, his mind starts to wander. It never bothered him before that he couldn't pray, but now that he has taken this step toward a better relationship with God, it bothers him a lot. Now John doesn't know what to do.

Have students pair up. Distribute paper and pencils as you explain: **John Lee is coming to you for some advice on how he can learn to pray better. What would you tell him to do? Write him an actual letter giving him some help. Make sure you use some of what we've learned today about creative prayers in Scripture.** Ask pairs to work for five minutes on their "Dear John" letters. Have several volunteers share what they suggested.

Option 3  Tough Questions

You'll need Several Bibles and this list of tough questions.

If your group needs to go a little deeper, here are some tough questions for them to wrestle with today. These questions are based on a story from the Bible where Jesus prayed using Scripture. Read Psalm 22:1-8,16-21 aloud, then explain:

Has anyone heard some of these words before? Do they remind you of anything else in the Bible? Jesus spoke some of these same words when He prayed on the cross. Let's take a look at that passage. Read Mark 15:21-39. **Psalm 22:14-18 also describes some of the events that took place at Jesus' crucifixion.** Discuss for a minute or two what these verses are describing.

1. **Why do you think Jesus thought of these words from the psalms at the point of His death?** The pattern of this psalm with its "suffering servant" message fits Jesus' experience perfectly; in fact, He was fulfilling prophecy here.

2. **Had God really forsaken Jesus, or did Jesus just feel forsaken?** With the weight of the sin of the world on Him, Jesus experienced true separation from His Father for the first time. It had to be this way for Him to die for our sins.

3. **One of the common languages spoken in Jesus' day was Aramaic. The writer of this gospel gives us Jesus' actual words in this language. Why do you think the writer used these words?** It shows the true impact of Jesus' emotion and His feelings of abandonment.

4. **What does it mean to pray in the Spirit?** It means to be in communion with the Holy Spirit or in the power of the Holy Spirit. The Holy Spirit is part of God's trinity, and often is seen as the One who guides and empowers us. The closer you are connected to God, the more likely that you will pray in His Spirit.

NOTES

STEP 4
MOVING OUT

This step allows students to experience Isaiah 6 as a powerful prayer.

Note: All three options in this step begin with the same creative experience, but the closing application in each option is different.

You'll need (for all three options) Three copies of "Isaiah 6 Dramatic Reading" (pp. 68-69), a Bible, a song leader with a guitar (or a CD player with appropriate CDs), and two students to be the narrators. The narrators need to have strong reading voices.

Ahead of time, have the narrators practice their parts to make this most effective.

Begin by turning the lights down to create a relaxed and intimate environment. Explain: **Today we're going to pray through a Scripture passage in Isaiah 6:1-8 so we'll all have to pay close attention and cooperate. We'll be doing all sorts of different types of prayer modeled in Scripture, like praying "popcorn prayers," meaning short one-word or one-sentence prayers, writing prayers on an overhead transparency and singing prayers together. Please close your eyes as we begin.** Let the narrators begin reading the Isaiah 6 script.

When the prayer is finished, conclude with one of the applications on the following page:

NOTES

Bible Bonus Note

Isaiah was a young man when he began his ministry. King Uzziah was likely one of his friends but once the king died, things got rough as enemy countries threatened to invade. God called Isaiah to do a tough job—talk straight to the people of Israel about what was wrong in their lives. Tradition and legend claim that Isaiah died a brutal death. Although the Bible doesn't explain this, it may be true. As you pray through Isaiah's words in Isaiah 6:1-8, keep in mind that the person who wrote it was a frightened young man—his friend the king was dead and other countries were threatening to invade the land.

Option 1  Light the Fire

You'll need An outdoor location, the plastic holder from a six-pack of soda, matches, a pan of water and a long (at least six-foot) piece of wire.

Ahead of time, practice the activity!

Using the wire, hang the plastic six-pack holder from a tree branch about five feet above the ground, placing the water dish below it. Light the plastic. As it starts to burn ,it will create small but really cool drops of plastic that sparkle and drop to the dish. While it's burning, ask students to think about how God would have them serve in the world and to commit themselves to serving Him.

Option 2  Fired Up

You'll need Several pieces of brightly colored three-hole-punched paper. **Note:** Pens or pencils are needed if you choose to do the suggested option.

Close your time together by asking students to talk about a typical day they have. Have them brainstorm about moments in their days when they can take a break and pray to God. One way to focus in our prayers and not get bored is to write them out.

Encourage students to write out a prayer each day during the same time—maybe before a class, when they first come home from school or before going to bed. Distribute a couple of sheets of colored paper to each student and instruct them to put the sheets in their school notebooks this week and write their prayers on them.

Option: If you have the time, have students write their first prayer right now.

Option 3  Spread the Fire

You'll need An overhead projector and screen (or a wall covered with blank poster paper), blank overhead transparency and transparency pens.

Try to maintain the prayerful mood from the "Isaiah 6 Dramatic Reading" as you explain: **Isaiah 6 leaves us at a place of commitment to say, "Here I am. Send me," just like Isaiah did.** Place a blank overhead transparency on the overhead projector and explain: **Let's write down places where we want God to send us to share about Him such as your school, neighborhood or maybe even your own home.** Instruct students to come up two at a time and write down places God might be sending them. Close in prayer that God will help us be like Isaiah whenever and wherever we can.

Tons of Types

Knowing that Ephesians 6:18 encourages us to pray in the Spirit on all occasions with all kinds of prayers and requests, circle any of the following that you have done while praying:

Talk out loud

Pray the same words together with others out loud

Talk in your own head to God

Keep a prayer journal

Lie flat on the ground

Sing

Kneel down

Say short prayers with a group of people

WRITE A LETTER TO GOD

Listen for a long period of silence

Lift your hands up in the air

Let's try one of those ways to pray to God right now by writing to Him. Take a moment to write a prayer to Him:

Dear God,

I think You're great because…

I confess that I've…

I really want to say thanks for…

I need help with…

Thanks, God!

Your friend,

Isaiah 6 Dramatic Reading

PART ONE

Narrator 1: *(Reading in a casual and relaxed manner)* In the year that King Uzziah died, I saw the Lord seated on a throne, high and exalted, and the train of His robe filled the temple. Above Him were seraphs, each with six wings; with two they covered their faces, with two they covered their feet, and with two they were flying. And they were calling out to one another.

Narrator 2: *(Also in a casual, relaxed manner)* Holy, holy, holy is the Lord Almighty; the whole earth is full of His glory.

Leader: *(that's you, the youth leader)* God, in our own minds, we too can see a vision of what Isaiah saw. We know that You are an amazing God. With these simple one-word prayers, Lord, we want to tell You that You are... *(At this point, let students fill in one-word or one-sentence phrases aloud describing who God is.)*

PART TWO

Narrator 1: *(Reading with some urgency and excitement, and starting over at verse 1)* In the year that King Uzziah died, I saw the Lord! He was seated on a throne, high and exalted, and the train of His robe filled the temple. Above Him were seraphs, each with six wings; with two they covered their faces, with two they covered their feet, and with two they were flying. And they were calling out to one another...

Narrator 2: *(Reading with the same urgency and excitement)* Holy, holy, holy is the Lord Almighty; the whole earth is full of His glory!

Narrator 1: *(Dramatically)* At the sound of their voices the doorposts and thresholds shook and the temple was filled with smoke.

Narrator 2: I am ruined! For I am a sinful man, and I live with sinful people, but now, my eyes have seen the King!

Leader: *(Lead, have the song leader lead, or play a song of confession. A good choice would be "Humble Thyself in the Sight of the Lord.")* God, we are such sinful people; we now confess to You that we have been... *(Then ask students to write one-word confessions—sins they've struggled with—on the overhead transparency by using a number of different-colored pens.)*

Part Three

Narrator 1: *(Quiet, fearful voice)* In the year that King Uzziah died, I saw the Lord! With Him were angelic beings who were calling out to one another…

Narrator 2: Holy, holy, holy is the Lord Almighty.

Narrator 1: At the sound of their voices the Temple shook and was filled with smoke.

Narrator 2: I am ruined! For I am a sinner.

Narrator 1: All of a sudden one angel flew to me with a live coal from the altar and touched my mouth with it.

Narrator 2: And he said, "See, your guilt is taken away and your sin has been paid for."

Leader: *(Lead a song of thankfulness for Jesus' forgiveness, such as "Jesus, Name Above All Names.")* Lord, we're nobody without You. Thank You for being such an incredible God. You've done so much for us. We now thank You for… *(Instruct students to come to the wall and write things they're thankful for on the poster paper.)*

Part Four

Narrator 1: In the year that King Uzziah died, I saw the Lord.

Narrator 2: And with Him were angelic beings, calling out to one another and saying, "Holy, holy, holy."

Narrator 1: I am ruined for I am a sinner. But one of the angels flew to me and said that my sin was paid for by someone else.

Narrator 2: Then I heard the voice of the Lord saying,

Narrator 1: *(Big voice)* "Who will go for us? Who shall I send into the world?"

Narrator 2: *(Quietly)* And I said, "Here I am, Lord. Send me."

Leader: *(Lead another worship song, possibly "Here I Am, Lord." After the song, explain that the final prayers will be sentence prayers.)* Lord, just like Isaiah, we're ready to be sent to do something big. But before we can go, we need Your help with some tough parts of our lives. Help us as we struggle with… *(Students call out sentence prayers.)*

Leader: In Jesus' name, we pray, amen.

Devotions in Motion

Week Four: What Can I Do When Prayer Gets Boring?

DAY 1

FAST FACTS

To see what it means to pray for others, quickly turn to 1 Samuel 12:20-25.

God Says

On your way to school you hear the news about a three-year-old who was accidentally shot in a drive-by a few blocks from your house. In history class your best friend tells you that her parents are getting divorced. During lunch you hear that your favorite teacher got in a car accident and was rushed to the hospital in an ambulance.

If you were Samuel, you would realize that the first thing you should do when you hear bad news is pray. Far be it from us that we should sin against others by not praying for them!

I Do

Think of three people who you know are having a tough time and spend a few minutes praying for each of them.

FOLD HERE --------------------------------

DAY 4

FAST FACTS

Do you ever get headaches? Want to know how to get rid of them? Then read James 5:13-16.

God Says

Finally the school bell rings and you hop on your bike and head for home. Since fifth period you've had a headache and you know your mom will know just what to do. After stashing your bike in your garage, you walk into your kitchen fully expecting your mom to be there to help with your headache. Unfortunately all that greets you is a note from your mom saying she'll be out running errands for the next couple of hours.

Just as you're trying to figure out what to do, you remember something you read in your Bible in James 5. "Aha," you think to yourself, "now I know just what to do." You grab the phone and call your best friend from church and ask him to pray for you.

I Do

The next time you're not feeling well, instead of reaching for aspirin, why don't you reach out and ask someone to pray with you?

Is there anybody you know who isn't feeling well today who you could call and pray with over the phone?

QUICK QUESTIONS

If you turn to Job 42:8-11, you'll see some of the funkiest names in the whole Bible.

God Says

Why did God want Job to pray for his friends?

☐ Because Job had an easier name to pronounce than Eliphaz the Temanite, Bildad the Shuhite and Zophar the Naamathite;

☐ Because Job hadn't sinned against God;

☐ Because Job could burp the alphabet out loud and no one else could.

What happened to Job and his friends because Job prayed for them?

I Do.

It's really important to pray for our friends who are distant from God. Name two friends who you know are far from God. Pray for them now and every time you think of them during the week.

QUICK QUESTIONS

To see how some of the first Christians acted, check out Acts 13:1-3.

God Says

True or False   The Holy Spirit spoke to the people as they were eating at an all-you-can-eat pizza restaurant.

True or False   They prayed that God would bless Barnabas's and Saul's work.

True or False   They placed their hands on Barnabas and Saul because they were trying to figure out who was more buff.

I Do.

Think of someone you know who is doing God's work. It might be your pastor at your church, your mom or your neighbor. Now take a few minutes to pray that God would bless his or her work today.

FOLD HERE

Pulse Prayer

The Big Idea

God answers every prayer in His own timing and in His own way.

Session Aims

In this session you will guide students to:

- Understand that God hears every prayer *and* answers every prayer;
- Accept God's answer even when it's different from what they want or expect;
- Begin to pray with the confidence that God will take care of them in the best way possible.

The Biggest Verse

"If my people, who are called by my name, will humble themselves and pray and seek my face and turn from their wicked ways, then will I hear from heaven and will forgive their sin and will heal their land." 2 Chronicles 7:14

Other Important Verses

2 Chronicles 7:14,15; Matthew 7:7-12

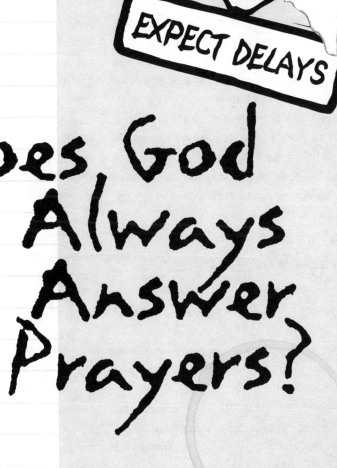

Does God Always Answer Prayers?

STEP

MOVING IN

This step introduces the idea that it's common to feel that nobody's listening to us.

Option 1  Move It

You'll need A VCR, TV and the video *Babe* cued approximately an hour and 15 minutes from the opening graphic to the scene where the dog is trying to get the sheep to listen to him.

Play the video clip for the group. After it's done, discuss: **We've all had times when we wonder if anybody is listening to us. Who can tell us about a time when you felt nobody was listening to you?** After a story or two (you may want to have a story ready yourself), explain: **In today's session we'll talk about how God always listens to us and always responds to us. Just as we saw as we studied Psalm 34, God reminds us that our humble attitude is key to His response to prayers. He'll always answer, but He seems especially responsive to people who know how much they need Him.**

Option 2  Chat Room

You'll need Copies of "Is Anybody Listening?" (p. 80) and pens or pencils.

Ahead of time, arrange for a student or adult volunteer to do something annoying at the start of your lesson, such as hum or tap a pencil. Explain that you will then ask him or her to be quiet. That works for a few seconds, but then the person should continue the annoying habit. Ask him or her to be quiet again, which again only works for a few seconds. Once the person continues the annoying habit for a third time, pretend to be really angry and yell: **Aren't you listening to me?**

Greet students, and begin to explain today's topic. (You'll have to ad lib here!) The person with the annoying habit should begin the first annoying sound just a few seconds

after you begin to speak. After you have finally yelled at that annoying person, make it clear to the other students that you had arranged this conflict ahead of time. But also make the point about how frustrating it is when you don't feel like anyone is listening to you.

Distribute the "Is Anybody Listening?" handouts and pens or pencils. Give students a few minutes to answer the questions on their own. When they're done, have them share the stories they wrote. Then ask the whole group the last question: **Do you think God ever stops listening to us? Why or why not?**

Transition to the rest of the lesson by explaining: **Today we're going to look at the truth about how God listens and responds to us.**

Option 3  Fun and Games

You'll need A silly prize for the winner (something from a thrift store or yard sale would work perfectly).

Divide students into groups of two, asking students to pair up with someone who's not their best friend. Person 1 in each pair has two minutes to tell the other person as many interesting and unusual things about herself as she can. Person 2 cannot say anything; he needs to simply listen as best he can. At the end of two minutes, have the listeners introduce their friends to the whole group by telling as much as they can remember about the person. When they're done, let Person 2 have two minutes to do the same for Person 1.

> **Hint:** If your group is larger than 10 people, you may need to divide them into smaller groups so that these introductions don't take too much time.

When everyone has been introduced, have a vote to see which person was the best overall listener and best at being able to recite information about the person they listened to. Award the prize to the "best listener."

Discuss: **Was it hard to just sit and listen for two minutes? Was it hard to remember everything the person told you? Why?**

Often we feel like we're talking, but nobody's listening. It's frustrating. Today we're going to take a look at how God, the great Listener, hears everything we say—*and remembers it all!*

STEP 2 — MOVING UP

This step teaches the truth that one of God's gifts to us is that He promises to always hear and always answer.

Option 1 — Move It

You'll need Several cans of Spam (canned ham), paper plates and several plastic knives.

Ask for approximately five volunteers. Explain that you'd like the volunteers to communicate about the best gift they've ever received, but that you have a special way you'd like them to communicate it. Hand them each a chunk of Spam on a paper plate and a plastic knife and ask them to carve out a replica of the best gift they've ever received. After giving them about 30 seconds to do this, hold up their Spam sculptures and ask students to guess what each masterpiece is.

Ask a student to read Matthew 7:7-11. Explain: **Can you imagine a good father giving his little kid a rock and a snake instead of food? Of course not; a good parent would want to give his child what he or she needs if he could. The passage tells us that if we ask, we will receive. God answers us, and not in the worst way possible, but in the best. God wants to give us great things! One of those great gifts is that He has promised to always answer our prayers.**

Have someone read 2 Chronicles 7:14,15. Summarize the verse for the group, then share a story about when God clearly answered one of your prayers. Ask students to share stories when they knew that God answered them as well.

Option 2 — Chat Room

You'll need Several Bibles, two fake tickets to the Super Bowl (or other similar event) and a wrapped present with a rubber snake and a rock in it.

Ahead of time, tell one of your adult leaders that you're going to be giving him a bogus gift at the meeting and that he should act surprised, then disappointed and a little angry because he was expecting something nice.

Share something like the following with the group: **Today's a really special moment. One of our leaders has been helping out now for two years, and we thought it would be a nice gesture to give him a special gift for his great efforts. Come on up, (Bob)! We thought really hard about what we should get him and we decided that since he loves to eat out, we'd get him this gift.** Have Bob come up to the front (looking all flustered and pleased) and open the gift, which of course is a total letdown. Patch things up by giving Bob the fake Super Bowl tickets instead.

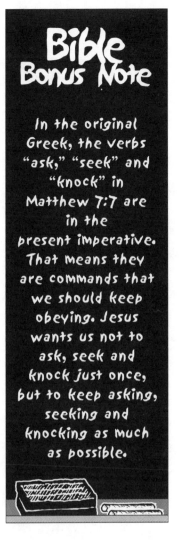

Bible Bonus Note

In the original Greek, the verbs "ask," "seek" and "knock" in Matthew 7:7 are in the present imperative. That means they are commands that we should keep obeying. Jesus wants us not to ask, seek and knock just once, but to keep asking, seeking and knocking as much as possible.

Does God Always Answer Prayer?

Ask: **Someone tell us about a time when you got a gift that was really weird. How did you feel after you opened the gift?**

Have a student read Matthew 7:7-12. Ask: **Can you imagine a good father giving his child a rock and a snake instead of food? Of course not; a good parent would want to please his child if he could. The passage tells us that if we ask, we will receive. God answers us, and not in the worst way possible, but in the best. God wants to give us great things!**

Have another student read 2 Chronicles 7:14,15. Explain: **The Bible gives us a pretty clear "if/then" statement:** *if* **we humble ourselves, try our best to follow God and take time to pray to Him,** *then* **He will answer us!**

Option 3  Pulse Points

You'll need Several Bibles, a rock, a rubber snake and something really meaningful you received as a gift once (hide the rock, snake and gift in a box or bag).

Ahead of time, ask a dad of one of the students to come to class and talk about how he does his best to take care of his family.

Spend a couple of minutes talking about one of the best gifts you ever received. After building it up, pull the snake and the rock out of the box or bag. Fake tears, if you can, over how meaningful these gifts were to you. Read Matthew 7:7-12 aloud and explain that there are three cool things we can learn from this passage:

1. A good dad gives good gifts.

Illustration: Ask the dad to share how he tries to provide the best he can for his family, even though it's often difficult.

2. The best dad gives the best gifts.

Illustration: Talk about the most meaningful gift that you received, showing everyone the gift and describing what it means to you, explaining: **That's the kind of gift God gives to us all the time.**

3. Our heavenly Dad gives the best gifts to those who stay humble toward Him.

Illustration: Ask the dad how his student's attitude makes a difference in how he responds to him or her. He always loves his kid, but perhaps he is more willing to respond to him or her when he or she comes to him with humility and a sense of neediness. Explain that the same is true of our God. Read 2 Chronicles 7:14,15 and explain: **God seems especially responsive to people who have become His people by asking Him to take over their lives. More than that, He seems responsive to His people who have decided to live humbly before Him and turn away from anything that keeps them from obeying Him.**

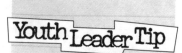

Youth Leader Tip

When working with junior highers, a great rule of thumb is to integrate families as much as possible. Families are still the primary place of influence in a junior higher's life, even more than church! So take advantage of any opportunity to invite parents to observe what you're doing. Or even better, make sure they participate in some way to get a real taste for your junior high ministry.

STEP 3 MOVING ON

This step teaches students that just because God always answers our prayers doesn't mean He always gives us what we want.

Option 1  Chat Room

You'll need A big chocolate bar or other inappropriate treat for a pet. Also have an alternate appropriate treat for the pet.

Ahead of time, arrange with one of the students to bring a pet—the weirder the better, but a dog or cat will be okay.

Introduce the student and his pet. Give him a minute to talk about the pet and its upkeep. Ask: **What do you do to take good care of your pet?** After his explanation, explain that you have a special treat for the pet, then pull out the huge chocolate bar (or something else that would be totally inappropriate for the pet). The pet owner will probably not be excited about the treat, even though the animal will want it. For example, chocolate may make dogs seriously ill. When the pet owner disagrees, make the point that the owner knows better than the pet what's best for it. (Give the appropriate treat to the pet.) Then discuss the following: **We're sort of like pets: we belong to God, who knows what's best for us.**

Can anyone give an example of a time when the answer God gave you seemed bad at the time but later turned out for the best?

How did you feel when you didn't get what you wanted? Sad, rejected, angry at God.

Why do you think what we want is often so different from what God wants for us? We see things from a self-centered perspective; He sees the whole perspective. We want what we think is best for us immediately; He thinks about what is best for us in the long run.

How would you feel about God if what you wanted was never what He wanted?

Could you still follow Him even if He never gave you what you wanted? Yes, you can as long as you remember that God is good; He can't do bad, so what He does for us is good.

Be prepared to share a story from your life when this happened to you.

Explain: **God answers our prayers, but not *always* in the way we want. He does, however, answer us in the way that's always best—even if we can't see it.**

Option 2  Real Life

You'll need Nothing, except this story.

This is a true story about a junior high kid:

Several years ago a seventh grader named John seemed to have the ideal life. He lived in Florida because his dad worked at Disney World. After school John and his friends would often hang out at the Magic Kingdom any time they wanted to! It was the perfect and ultimate junior high life!

Then one day it all changed. John's dad took a new job and they had to move to a completely different place—northern Maine! He thought the world had ended; there was no more Disney World and there was a new thing called "snow and ice" to deal with. For the first few days John was miserable. He thought about running away. He punished his dad through bad behavior; it was his only way of striking back at the injustice he felt.

But then an amazing thing happened. At the school John went to, he met the friendliest kids he had ever known. Within several weeks he realized that he actually had better friends than he had had where he used to live. Now John is happy for the move and wouldn't want to go back!

Ask for students to share stories when they felt like they were given a raw deal, only to discover later that it was all for the best. To help them think of stories, ask if anyone has had a tough medical situation in their family that they struggled with. Often we find that good comes out of tough medical situations. Conclude this step by saying that even when it seems God has not heard our prayers, He answers us by giving us something that in the long run is much better.

Option 3  Tough Questions

You'll need Nothing, except these questions.

Talk about a recent world tragedy (hurricane, earthquake, etc.). Discuss the following:

1. **Do you think the people who experienced this disaster were praying for it not to happen? Does this mean that God doesn't answer prayers?** No, it means that the world is not perfect and has evil things present—and sometimes tragic things happen. But God works through the tragedy to help people.

2. **Why does God allow things like this to happen?** God didn't set up a puppet world where everything is simple and easy. He set up a world where bad things can happen because that's the only way really good things can happen too. Isn't it nice that your dog loves you just because he loves you, and not because you make him love you?

3. **Since the Bible says if we ask, we'll receive, doesn't that mean we can pray for anything and get it?** No, because God is truly concerned for our overall welfare and not just our wants. He knows what we need. He wants us to ask for the things we need—like the bread and fish in the Matthew 7:9,10. The Bible doesn't ever mention anything about a nice Porsche on your sixteenth birthday.

STEP 4 MOVING OUT

This step enables students to pray this week, knowing that God will hear and answer.

Option 1  Light the Fire

You'll need Small fish symbols (from a local Christian bookstore, or you can make your own out of paper or self-adhesive labels), one for each student.

Distribute the fish symbols to students, mentioning that this was an ancient symbol for Christians to identify themselves to each other. Reflect on Matthew 7:9,10 again and that when we ask for a fish we don't get a stone. Have students put the fish symbol on their key chains or in their pockets, notebooks or backpacks to remind them that when they pray this week, God answers. Encourage them: **His answer might not be what we immediately want, but it will always be the best thing for us.**

Option 2  Fired Up

You'll need 3x5-inch index cards, a hat (or box or basket) and pens or pencils.

Distribute the index cards and pens or pencils and have students write their names on their cards and their biggest prayer need or request that they wouldn't mind others knowing about. Collect the cards and place them in the hat (or box or basket), then have students one at a time draw out a card (not their own of course) and put it in a safe place. Instruct students to keep the request private and encourage them to pray every day this week for the person whose card they picked. Sometime during the week call each student to remind them to pray for the other person. Remind them that everyone has someone praying for him or her, and since God answers prayer and answers it with our best interests in mind, something great is going to happen.

In a week or two, have students share any answers to their prayers. They can expect God to do something!

Option 3  Spread the Fire

You'll need Paper, pens or pencils and masking or transparent tape.

Explain: **Just as prayers often work out differently than we expect, God often causes people to know Him in ways that are different from what we expect. I'm curious; how did you come to know God?** Write students' responses on the different pieces of paper. Answers may include: fear of going to hell, something painful in their life, their family, the need to have a friend, the witness of a friend, had a crush on someone who went to church, etc. Tape these pieces of paper to the door (or the wall next to it) and explain: **There are many doors to get to the one true Jesus.** Ask each student to pray for at least one friend who doesn't know Jesus yet—that their friend will find the right door to get to Him!

NOTES

Is Anybody Listening?

Think back to a time when you felt nobody was listening to you. Describe the situation:

Now think about a time when you weren't listening to someone else. Describe this situation:

Did you feel guilty about not listening?

What was the response of the other person?

Think back to a tough time in your life when you felt God wasn't listening either. Describe this situation:

Was this a frustrating time for you?

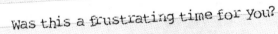

How did it make you feel about God?

Do you think God ever stops listening? Why or why not?

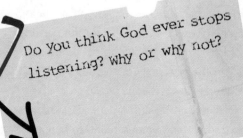

Devotions in Motion

WEEK FIVE: DOES GOD ALWAYS ANSWER PRAYERS?

CONSTRUCTION ZONE

EXPECT DELAYS

DAY 1

QUICK QUESTIONS

If you'd like to hear an answer from God today, flip to 1 Samuel 3:1-21.

God Says

Samuel was close to your age when he heard from God. How would you feel if you heard God talking to you?

How do you think God would be most likely to speak to you?

- ☐ A web page on the internet
- ☐ A voice that you could actually hear
- ☐ A slick infomercial, complete with his own 1-800 number
- ☐ Stories in the Bible
- ☐ Your pet turtle (turtles can do amazing tricks, you know)
- ☐ Other people who know him
- ☐ A daytime talk show
- ☐ Through his Holy Spirit

I Do

Spend a few minutes today asking God a few questions. See how He might answer you today, whether it be through an audible voice or just a sense of what he wants you to do.

DAY 4

QUICK QUESTIONS

Is praying once for something enough? Well, sometimes, but sometimes not, as Luke 18:1-8 will show you.

God Says

Why did the widow get the justice she wanted?

Why do you think faith is important in our prayers?

I Do

Is your attitude toward prayer more like a candy Gobstopper, meaning you pray once and it lasts forever, or more like a breath mint, meaning you need to keep praying lots of times each and every day?

What is one thing you can pray about every day for the next week?

Pulse

DAY 2

FAST FACTS

The story in Daniel 3:1-27 might seem a little long, but it's worth the four minutes it will take you to read it.

God Says

Imagine you could tap into Shadrach's brain. Here's what he might be thinking:

Boy, I sure am afraid. I'd like to live after all, but that fire sure looks hot. I'm sweating up a storm already. But Meshach is sweating more than me. I can smell him all the way over here. I'd hate to see my clothes catch on fire, especially the new shirt that I'm wearing. Good thing I've got God on my side. He'll answer my prayers. He might not save me from the fire, but He'll do what's best. Whew-ee, that Meshach sure does smell!

I Do

Shadrach undoubtedly was a little afraid. After all, he was human. But he knew that God would answer his prayer, even if it was a different answer than he was hoping for. Make sure you thank God today that even though His answers may be different from what you expect, He'll always do the best thing for you.

DAY 3

FAST FACTS

Before you do anything else, read Mark 14:32-36.

God Says

The school banquet is coming up, and you've already gotten a new dress for it. You've figured out how to wear your hair, and you even have matching shoes. Only one problem: you are hoping to go with this guy, Harry, who has a locker near yours, but he hasn't asked you quite yet. You're sure he will though. After all, you've prayed about it every day for the last month.

The Tuesday before the dance you find out that Harry asked Amy to go. That doesn't make sense. Why didn't God do what you wanted Him to do?

I Do

As we see in Mark 14:32-36, the key is not to ask for our own will, but God's will to be done. God's answers to prayer always match what He wants, not necessarily what we want. Think of two things you can pray about today by following Jesus' example of asking for God's will, not your own, to be done.

FOLD HERE

Prayer

The Big Idea

Persistence and practice are good things—especially when it comes to praying.

Session Aims

In this session you will guide students to:

- Recognize that praying is like anything they want to do well—it takes practice;
- Experience closeness to God because they are praying more often;
- Commit to praying more frequently this week.

The Biggest Verse

"Jesus told his disciples...that they should always pray and not give up." Luke 18:1

Other Important Verses

Luke 11:5-8; 18:1-8; 1 Thessalonians 5:17-9

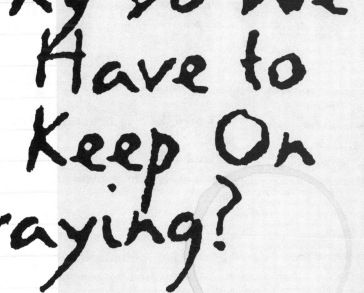

Why Do We Have to Keep On Praying?

STEP

MOVING IN

This step introduces the idea that it's easy to practice things we enjoy.

Option 1  Move It

You'll need Students who can play musical instruments.

   Ahead of time, ask students who play musical instruments to bring them and prepare to play "Happy Birthday."

Greet students and ask for any of them who were born in the present month to come to the front of the room. Then call up the students who have brought their musical instruments and lead a rousing version of the song "Happy Birthday." Now ask the student musicians to switch instruments with someone else and play "Happy Birthday" one more time. Since virtually nothing sounds worse than junior highers playing instruments they don't know how to play, your second version is sure to sound awful.

   Ask the student musicians: **What was the difference between the first and second versions? How did you each get so good at playing your instruments?** The answer is (hopefully!) they practiced and persisted—maybe even at times when they didn't feel like it. Explain: **Today we're going to look at prayer and see how practicing prayer will help us communicate better with God.**

Option 2  Chat Room

You'll need Copies of "Talent Time" (p. 90), pens or pencils and two or three folding tables.

   Ahead of time, ask students to bring art creations, musical instruments or demonstrations of any of their special hobbies. Set up the tables for students to display their things.

As students arrive, have them spread out their creations on the display tables. Begin the meeting by asking students to share what they brought and talk about how their interest began. Ask them how much time this activity/creation takes to do and if they enjoy the time they spend on it or if they find it a chore.

   After everyone has shared, compliment them on their efforts and talent and explain: **When we find things we like to do and enjoy working on, it's really not tough to spend the time and energy on them.**

   Distribute copies of "Talent Time" and pens or pencils. Allow a couple of minutes to complete the handout, then divide students into small groups of three to five and have them share their answers with each other.

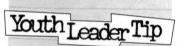

Merely mentioning to students to bring items will result in one thing: no items brought. You'll need to encourage students individually both in person and on the phone to make sure they bring their things. With junior highers, a phone call means everything. In fact, if you call every kid in your group (or have other adult leaders call), you will be stunned at the response!

When the small groups are finished, bring the whole group back together. Ask students to point to the person in their small group discussion who has the most unusual talents or hobbies, then have that student share with the whole group what he/she told the small group. After everyone is done, emphasize that most people are good at things they work hard at, particularly when they enjoy the time they spend. Then explain: **I noticed nobody said that "prayer" was one of their talents or interests. But in this session we're going to look at prayer a little differently. It is something we can actually enjoy doing, and if we do it a lot, amazing things just might happen in our lives.**

Option 3  Fun and Games

You'll need A standard folding rectangular table and a $10 bill. (A $100 bill would be even better if you happen to be an independently wealthy youth leader, and yes, there's a chance you won't be getting it back!).

Ahead of time, set up the table in the front of the room, away from the wall, (ideally with carpet or other padding under it) and arrange for two leaders (or strong junior highers) to each hold down an end.

Pull the $10 bill out of your pocket. Challenge any student to do the following for the money: **Begin by sitting on top of the table; then climb over the side edge, under the table and back up the other side, without touching the floor or the table legs.** Very few students will be able to do this (a sixth-grade gymnast comes to mind) but your group will have a lot of fun watching them try. Several will be very frustrated that they can't seem to do it and they'll try many times. After several have tried to accomplish the feat, let them try to do it in pairs.

When they've tried the stunt for a few minutes, congratulate their efforts and explain: **Some of you amazed me at your willingness to try and try again. Persistence pays off! It never hurts to work at something as hard as you can and try your best. Believe it or not, that's even true when we're talking to God in prayer.**

STEP 2 — MOVING UP

This step helps students wrestle with whether or not God will change His mind if we bug Him enough.

Option 1  Move It

You'll need Several Bibles and three copies of the script "Bread at Midnight" (pp. 91-92).

Ahead of time, choose three people to act out this short play. No props are needed, but people with comic timing would be helpful! Give them each a copy of the script and time to rehearse, *ideally* a few days before the meeting. Memorizing it would be best, though reading the script will be fine too.

After the play is over, thank the actors. Then read the passage as it's written in Luke 11:5-8 and ask: **It's kind of an unusual story, isn't it? It sounds like if you bug someone enough, they'll cooperate. Do you think that's true with God? Why wouldn't God answer the first time?** Well, God could answer the first time, but He often chooses to answer after we have prayed repeatedly because that shows that we know we need to depend on Him.

Option 2  Chat Room

You'll need Several Bibles in various translations.

Read the following questions, and instruct students to move to the left side of the room if they are more bugged by the first kind of person or to the right side of the room if they are more bugged by the second kind of person.
What bugs you more...
Someone who never stops talking, or someone who never listens?
Someone who comes to your house to give you a ride to church and always comes early, or someone who always comes late?
The teacher's pet, or the school bully?
Someone who has you on her E-mail "buddy list"

this before option 1

and always wants to chat with you while you're on-line even when you don't want to talk to her, or someone who never answers your E-mail?
Someone who yawns without covering his mouth, or someone who sneezes without covering her nose and mouth?
Someone who asks you for paper every day in history, or someone who asks you for part of your lunch every day?

Transition from the last question by explaining: **We all get bugged when people keep asking us for stuff. Today we're going to read a story about someone in the Bible who kept asking for stuff he needed.** Distribute the Bibles and ask several students to read Luke 11:5-8 from the different versions. Then do the same with Luke 18:1-8. Have students turn to the person next to them and discuss the following question for 30 seconds: If the friend in the house and the judge represent God, what do these two stories tell us about Him? After 30 seconds, ask students to share their answers.

Allow 30 more seconds each for pairs to answer the following questions, taking time between each one to discuss the answers as a group:
If the friend who needs bread and the persistent widow represent us, what do these two stories tell us about ourselves?
What do these two stories teach us about prayer?

Conclude by asking the entire group: **So, is bugging God until He finally gives in the key to prayer? If not, what is Jesus talking about?** Jesus is talking about our need to repeatedly seek God for things, because even though He could answer our prayers the first time we asked (or even before we asked for that matter), the more times we ask Him, the greater our sense of need for Him. The more the widow asked the judge, the more desperate she became for his help. The same is true in our relationship with God today.

Option 3 — Pulse Points

You'll need A quarter, some candy prizes and a student volunteer.

Ahead of time, arrange for the volunteer to interrupt you a few seconds into the session by bugging you for a quarter. Have him continue to bug you until you finally give in.

Share a story of a person who accomplished something because of great persistence and dedication (for ideas, check any issue of *Sports Illustrated* or *Guideposts* magazine). Have your "plant" student raise his or her hand at an inappropriate time and ask if they can borrow a quarter, then keep on bothering you about it until you finally give in and hand him a quarter just to shut him up! Finish the story, mentioning something about the persistence of both the lead character in the story and the student who interrupted, then read Luke 11:5-8 aloud.

Explain: **An incorrect understanding of this story is to think that if we bug God, He'll eventually give in. Instead, here are two correct truths we can learn from Jesus' story.**

86

1. Good Prayer Asking

Illustration: **The friend who needed bread knew exactly where to go for help. Do you know where to go for help in this room?** At this point, show the candy prizes and explain that whoever gets to where they need to go first to find each of the following items will get a prize:

- Where you keep the Bibles;
- Where to find pencils;
- Where your secret candy stash is hidden;
- Whatever else is appropriate to the room.

Explain: **The friend who needed bread knew that God was the place to go to find what he needed. Good prayer asking means going to God to get help with what we need. And often it means going to God many, many times.**

2. Good Prayer Answering

Read Luke 18:1-8.

Illustration: **God always provides for our needs. This doesn't mean He always provides for our "wants,"** however. Help students distinguish needs from wants by explaining: **God will provide our needs for food, drink, clothes and shelter, but that doesn't necessarily mean we'll be sipping a chocolate shake and eating a hamburger while lounging on the deck of our beautiful yacht.**

Conclude by telling the students about a time when you found yourself praying with boldness and persistence for some issue in your life and what happened as a result.

NOTES

STEP 3 MOVING ON

This step helps students realize that persistent prayer is not about bugging God, but about practicing—just as we do with other activities that we enjoy—and about developing a better friendship with God.

Option 1 Chat Room

You'll need Several Bibles.

Ask students to close their eyes for a moment and concentrate on what they're doing right now that they rarely think about. Ask them to call out ideas—for example, "I notice my breathing," "I feel my heart pounding," "I feel hot," "I'm falling asleep." Now have them open their eyes. Ask: **What would happen if we had to think every moment about breathing or keeping our hearts beating? What makes us do these things without having to think about them?**

Now read 1 Thessalonians 5:17. Discuss for a moment the phrase, "pray continually." Ask: **Is this possible? Can we really pray all the time?**

Spend a couple of moments talking about how great it would be if we could pray just like we breathe. It's possible. God wants us to be so in tune with Him that we think about Him and talk to Him every moment we can. Ask: **Does anyone here find himself talking out loud to God sometimes when no one else is around? What is that experience like?**

Talking to God at any and all times is a great thing to do. It might look weird to people around you, but God loves it. And the more you practice praying this way, the more it's like anything you're good at: you'll enjoy it more and you'll be better at it. You'll also be blown away by the things that start to happen.

Ask: **What kind of things might happen if you pray constantly?** Answers might include: you'll see more prayers answered and/or you'll be thinking more about God. The important thing to stress here is that our relationship with God becomes stronger as we practice praying.

Option 2 — Real Life

You'll need The book *The Practice of the Presence of God* by Brother Lawrence (Washington, D. C.: ICS Publications, 1994).

Ahead of time, read through the book and be prepared to briefly share his story, possibly reading one of the letters out loud to students.

Share your own outline of the book or use the following if you didn't have time to skim the book:

I want to tell you a true story of a guy who lived a long time ago. His name was Larry, and he found himself always struggling between the times when he was serving God and the times when he was not thinking about God at all. He would feel so guilty about ignoring God that he'd pray for long periods to ask for forgiveness. When he felt forgiven, he'd find himself thinking about how proud he was that he could be so humble as to ask forgiveness, then he'd realize he was now sinning again and would have to go back to God in prayer! His life was a continual battle between struggling in prayer and ignoring God.

For years Larry struggled with this battle, but he slowly came to realize that the solution for him was to begin to "practice the presence of prayer" all the time. In other words, Larry wanted to be in continual communication with God at every moment instead of back and forth between praying and ignoring God. He taught himself to be in this state of mind and it became the key to his life. Rarely did he struggle anymore because he had practiced his way into a new relationship with God.

Explain: **What makes this story interesting is that Larry was actually Brother Lawrence, a monk who lived in a monastery and devoted his life to serving God.**

We don't live in monasteries, but we can practice the same thing he did. Close your eyes for a moment and see what comes into your mind. Whatever it is: It might be school, a friend, someone you have a crush on, anything. Now bring God into the picture: ask Him to help that friend, to be with you at school, to let the person you have a crush on know about it! Bring God into your images. It's hard to just think about God, so think about how God is involved with all the other things your mind likes to dwell on. That's practicing the presence of God.

Close by reading 1 Thessalonians 5:17, then explain: **"Pray continually"; that's the Bible's way to say it. It's not about bugging God until He answers but praying with an attitude that says we're going to pray with persistence and boldness. We'll grow so much closer to God when we pray this way.**

Option 3 — Tough Questions

You'll need Just your Bible and these questions!

Read 1 Thessalonians 5:17, then discuss the following:

1. **Have you ever felt guilty because you knew you should have prayed for something but forgot to and something bad happened? Is it actually your fault that the "something bad" happened?** God is still sovereign over everything; we don't have to take responsibility for bad things happening just because we forgot to pray.

2. **Do disasters in the world happen because people have stopped praying?** If that were the case, wouldn't the world have no problems at all if someone were praying 24 hours a day? Bad things happen because sin, evil and Satan exist in this world. Since the world is not perfect and good, there will always be some tough things happening. But prayer can help us through the tough things.

3. **Do you think God ever gets a little irritated that some people pray too much, for example a person who prays 30 minutes for a parking space? Why or why not?** Well, praying for 30 minutes for a parking space isn't necessarily a bad thing, but there are more important things that we could be praying about, such as our friends who don't know Jesus yet or different situations we hear about in the news that need God's help.

4. **Isn't praying without ceasing just another one of those impossible things God told us to do?** No, it's another one of the Bible's statements that is purposely overstated to make the point; no one can pray at every moment (what happens when you sleep?), but we can certainly develop an attitude of prayer during most of our waking moments.

STEP 4

MOVING OUT

This step enables students to practice praying more this week.

Option 1 — Light the Fire

You'll need Dr. Seuss's *Horton Hears a Who* (New York: Random House Books for Young Readers, 1954, 1966).

Let everyone get comfortable as you tell them you're going to read a really intense story. Then pull out Dr. Seuss and enjoy reading it. When you're done, mention how Horton's persistence paid off! Explain: **In a similar way, when we're persistent in our prayers to God, it pays off. God loves to hear us pray frequently and boldly.** Close with a brief time of prayer, asking God to help us practice praying at every available moment.

Option 2 — Fired Up

You'll need Postcards and a list of students' addresses.

Gather the group in a circle and hold hands. Sing an appropriate praise song that includes words about prayer (the round "Love, Love, Love, Love, Christians This Is Your Call" or "Father, I Adore You" would be good choices). When the singing is done, pray that God would keep the song ringing in everybody's head for the next few days, so that every time they think of that song, they would be reminded to pray about something and learn more about praying continually.

The day after the meeting, mail a postcard to everyone that simply says: "'Father, I adore You,' (or whatever song you chose). Are you still praying?"

Three days later mail another that says: "'Father, I'm still adoring You.' Keep on praying until the next time I see you!"

Option 3 — Spread the Fire

You'll need Nothing!

Close the session with an encouraging word about praying continually. To help them practice this, wrap up with a prayer asking all the students to leave their eyes open and converse easily with God as if He's a close friend. Instead of saying "Amen," say "Good-bye" to everyone and tell them the prayer has not ended. Explain that this week, when they see friends or neighbors or teachers at school, they should say a quick prayer for those people. Encourage them to pray specifically that those people would come to know Jesus as Savior. Then the next time your group is together, begin the meeting by saying "Amen!" and remind students that they just finished a 168-hour prayer!

NOTES

Talent Time

1. Make a list of your best talents:

2. Make a list of things you enjoy doing:

3. Make a list of things you spend a lot of time doing, but you don't really like to do:

Now go back to the first question. Look at the items you listed. Why are you so good at doing these things?

Now go back to the second question. What is it that you like best about these things?

Why do you spend so much time doing the things listed in the third question?

Will it turn out best in the long run that you had to work hard on these? Why or why not?

Now, draw a picture of your youth leader, so he or she can determine quickly if you have much drawing talent.

BREAD AT MIDNIGHT

BASED ON LUKE 11:5-8

Narrator: Once upon a time there were two friends. (*Two friends enter, eyeing each other suspiciously.*) One friend said to the other:

Friend 1: You're my friend.

Friend 2: You're my friend too.

Friend 1: You're my best friend.

Friend 2: What is it you need this time? (*He says with suspicion.*)

The two friends separate as though going to their own homes. Friend 2 lies down and falls asleep.

Narrator: One evening at about midnight...

Friend 2: I knew it.

Narrator: Friend 1 went to Friend 2 and said:

Friend 1: Hey buddy!

Friend 2: ZZZZZ (*and other heavy sleeping noises*).

Friend 1: Hey buddy, I know you're up there!

Friend 2: ZZZZZ (*and other even heavier sleeping noises*).

Friend 1: You're my best friend, you know!

Narrator: Finally Friend 2 answered his best friend:

Friend 2: (*To narrator*) I never said he was my best friend.

Narrator: Finally Friend 2 answered his friend:

Friend 2: Criminy! Do you know what time it is?

Friend 1: (*Looks at watch*) About 5 P.M.—in New York.

Friend 2: This ain't New York, pal. It's midnight!

Friend 1: So it is.

Friend 2: So go to bed.

Friend 1: I'd like to; there's just one thing I need.

Narrator: Friend 2 was completely exasperonerated.

Friend 2: (*To Narrator*) Huh?

Narrator: Anyway, he was not thrilled about doing anything at midnight except sleeping.

Friend 2: Look, I'm going back to sleep. The door's locked—we keep it locked ever since you tried this stunt last month—and my kids are in bed with me and I don't want to wake them up.

Friend 1: What are your kids doing in bed with you?

Friend 2: The bunk beds fell apart.

Friend 1: Oh. Well, it's not going to kill you to give me a hand. You see, my Uncle Morty just showed up with his six kids and wouldn't you know it, we ran out of food. All I need is three loaves of bread, and I'd appreciate it if it wasn't as crusty as the stuff I borrowed last month.

Narrator: Friend 2 decided to blow his friend/mooch/acquaintance off and go back to sleep. A few uncomfortable moments passed.

Pause for five seconds.

Friend 1: (*Howling like a wolf*) Aaahhhoooow! (*Pause, meows like a cat, pause*) Yabba dabba doo! (*Pause, scream anything from a current TV commercial that the audience knows!*)

Friend 2: Criminy! Bug off pal!

Friend 1: Four score and seven years ago, our forefathers...

Friend 2: Stop it!

Friend 1: (*Singing*) Kum Ba Ya, my Lord...

Friend 2: That's it! If you want your bread so badly, I'll get it!

Friend 1: You are a great friend. I'll never forget this! By the way, what's criminy mean?

Friend 2 just shrugs shoulders and pretends to throw bread to Friend 1.

Narrator: So Friend 2 threw some bread out the window.

Friend 1: Cool. You couldn't spare some mayo, too, could you?

Friend 2 throws a pillow (or similar object) at Friend 1. Friend 1 leaves.

Narrator: And so the persistent Friend 1 was able to feed his uncle Morty at midnight. It all just goes to show you three important lessons about life: never buy your children's furniture at Bob's Furniture World; choose your friends wisely, and if you need something, be really, really persistent. The end.

Devotions in Motion

WEEK SIX: WHY DO WE HAVE TO KEEP ON PRAYING?

DAY 1

FAST FACTS

To find out what Jesus did even before He washed His face and brushed His teeth, flip open to Mark 1:35.

God Says

It's dark outside. The sun's not even up yet. Everyone around Him is still asleep. Instead of singing some obnoxious good morning song to wake everyone up, He heads out of the house and goes off to a nearby hill where He spends time with God and where He hears from His Father.

Who's the He we're talking about? It's Jesus. Since Jesus was God, He could do anything He wanted and what He wanted to do most was pray. He knew that He needed time every day with God the Father.

I Do

Just like Jesus, we need to keep on praying not to get what we think we want, but to get what we ultimately need most—a closer friendship with God. Right now ask God to help you have a closer friendship with Him and to help you develop that friendship like Jesus did—by spending time in prayer.

FOLD HERE

DAY 4

FAST FACTS

If you like to talk, Colossians 4:2-6 will really help you out.

God Says

For the last few weeks you and your stepmom have been praying for your new neighbors. They don't seem to be Christians, and you're praying that God would give you a chance to share with them about Jesus.

One Thursday afternoon you come home from school and find your stepmom talking with one of the new neighbors in your own living room. Your stepmom says hello. Then asks why you didn't clean your room that morning. Before you know it, you start yelling back at your stepmom. "What do you mean why didn't I clean my room? I was running late this morning. Plus it's not that dirty. I wish you'd just leave me alone. You're not my real mom anyway." Then you storm up to your room, slamming the door behind you.

A few minutes later you start to feel bad. That wasn't a very good way to treat your stepmom, not to mention the fact that the neighbor you've been praying for saw you. If you had been praying more the last few days, maybe you would have done a better job of controlling your mouth.

I Do

One of the best ways we can share with others about Jesus is through our words; yet we often say some really lame and mean things. Getting our tongues under control is a daily battle. Ask God to help you use your tongue for good stuff, not bad stuff, this week.

QUICK QUESTIONS

If you want to find out about your worst enemy (and no, we don't mean brussels sprouts), head to Ephesians 6:10-18.

Who is your worst enemy?

God Says

☐ The alarm clock that wakes you up in the morning

☐ The big bad wolf

☐ The devil

☐ The boogey man

What are the six parts of the armor that God gives us to help us fight the devil?

Why is prayer important in this armor (see v. 18)?

I Do.

Think of an area in your life where the devil is trying to tempt you or drag you away from God. Visualize yourself wearing all six parts of the armor and then pray that God would help you stand against the devil's plans against you. You might need to do this over and over again maybe even every day, because the devil never stops trying to mess you up.

FOLD HERE

QUICK QUESTIONS

To find out more of Paul's reasons to keep on praying, check out Philippians 4:4-7.

What is the command in Philippians 4:6?

God Says

What happens once you pray?

☐ A seven-foot-long banana split will appear next to you.

☐ Your mom will eliminate your chores for the rest of the year.

☐ You'll have peace and you won't worry anymore.

You could probably think of something to worry about every single day. What does this say about why we need to keep on praying?

I Do.

What are two things you are worried about right now? Pray about them and experience God's amazing peace.

HOW DO I PRAY?

Prayer is like a phone call to a best friend. There's not an actual phone or phone cord, but it's like a direct line for talking to God whenever we want to. We can talk for just a few minutes or a few hours. And unlike our normal phone calls that can get busy signals or not be answered because no one is home, God's line is always open. He's always right there waiting for us to call Him. No matter where we go, we can always talk to Jesus. God cares for us so much that He's always listening.

WHY SHOULD WE PRAY?

- Because when we want to get to know someone, we hang out with them or call them on the phone. It's the same with Jesus. We can get to know Him by spending time talking to Him about whatever we want to.
- Because God loves us and wants to know our needs.
- Because we can ask God for His direction for our lives or what He wants us to do.

If we want Jesus to be our best friend, we need to talk to Him; then we'll learn exactly what He wants us to do.

On the Move

HOW DO WE PRAY?

- We can pray with other people or we can pray alone.
- God knows our thoughts—so we don't have to pray out loud if we don't want to.
- We don't have to close our eyes, but we may want to so that we're not distracted.
- Lifting our hands shows praise and a willing heart to do what God wants us to do.
- Kneeling during prayer shows honor and respect to God.
- Lying on the floor shows complete surrender and humbleness toward God.

We don't have to kneel or lift our hands or even speak out loud for God to hear us. Because God loves us so much, we know that God hears us no matter when, how or where we pray.

WHAT CAN WE PRAY ABOUT?

- Just like talking with our best friend, we can include God in every area of our lives.
- We can tell Him all of our secrets, problems and needs, and ask Him for help.
- We can thank Him for the answers to our prayers.
- We can praise Him for His goodness, blessings and love.

Prayer is our own special line to God. As we learn to trust God with more and more of our lives through prayer, we learn something else—we don't have to hang up our end of the line either! We can keep our line open, talking to our best friend—24-7.

PIPING HOT RESOURCES FOR YOUTH WORKERS

**Games, Crowdbreakers
and Community Builders**
Jim Burns, Mark Simone & Joel Lusz
Manual / 219p • ISBN 08307.18818 • $16.99

Skits & Dramas
Jim Burns, General Editor
Manual / 172p • ISBN 08307.18826 • $16.99

Bible Study Outlines and Messages
Jim Burns & Mike DeVries
Manual / 219p • ISBN 08307. 18850 • $16.99

**Illustrations, Stories and Quotes
to Hang Your Message On**
Jim Burns & Greg McKinnon
Manual / 237p • ISBN 08307.18834 • $16.99

Worship Experiences
Jim Burns & Robin Dugall
Manual / 144p • ISBN 08307.24044 • $16.99

Missions and Service Projects
Jim Burns, General Editor
Manual / 121p • ISBN 08307.18796 • $16.99

Incredible Retreats
Jim Burns & Mike DeVries
Manual / 144p • ISBN 08307.24036 • $16.99

**Case Studies, Talk Sheets
and Discussion Starters**
Jim Burns & Mark Simone
Manual / 125p • ISBN 08307.18842 • $16.99

Nobody Talks Your Teens' Language Like Jim Burns

YouthBuilders Group Bible Studies are a high-involvement, discussion-oriented, Bible-centered, comprehensive program
for seeing teens through their high-school years and beyond. From respected youth worker Jim Burns. Reproducible!

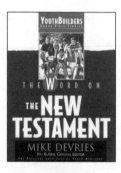

The Word on the Old Testament
Manual / 135p
ISBN 08307.17269 • $16.99

The Word on the New Testament
Manual / 170p
ISBN 08307.17250 • $16.99

The Word on Spiritual Warfare
ISBN 08307.17242 • $16.99

The Word on the Basics of Christianity
Manual / 245p
ISBN 08307.16440 • $16.99

The Word on the Sermon on the Mount
Manual / 148p
ISBN 08307.17234 • $16.99

The Word on Sex, Drugs & Rock 'N' Roll
Manual / 186p
ISBN 08307.16424 • $16.99

The Word on Family
ISBN 08307.17277 • $16.99

The Word on Helping Friends in Crisis
Manual / 223p
ISBN 08307.16467 • $16.99

**The Word on Finding
and Using Your Spiritual Gifts**
Manual / 203p
ISBN 08307.17897 • $16.99

The Word on Prayer and the Devotional Life
Manual / 213p
ISBN 08307.16432 • $16.99

**The Word on Being a Leader,
Serving Others & Sharing Your Faith**
Manual / 195p
ISBN 08307.16459 • $16.99

The Word on the Life of Jesus
Manual / 195p
ISBN 08307.16475 • $16.99

Available at your local Christian bookstore.

Gospel Li

04